Big Steps for Little People

of related interest

Understanding Looked After Children
Psychology for Foster Care
Jeune Guishard-Pine, Suzanne McCall and Lloyd Hamilton
Foreword by Andrew Wiener
ISBN 978 1 84310 370 7

Fostering Attachments
Supporting Children who are Fostered or Adopted
Kim S. Golding
ISBN 978 1 84310 614 2

Creating Loving Attachments
Parenting with PACE to Nurture Confidence and Security in the Troubled Child
Kim S. Golding and Daniel A. Hughes
ISBN 978 1 84905 227 6

Living Alongside a Child's Recovery
Therapeutic Parenting with Traumatized Children
Billy Pughe and Terry Philpot
Foreword by Mary Walsh, co-founder and Chief Executive of SACCS
ISBN 978 1 84310 328 8

First Steps in Parenting the Child who Hurts
Tiddlers and Toddlers
2nd edition
Caroline Archer
ISBN 978 1 85302 801 4

Next Steps in Parenting the Child Who Hurts
Tykes and Teens
Caroline Archer
ISBN 978 1 85302 802 1

Connecting with Kids through Stories
Using Narratives to Facilitate Attachment in Adopted Children
2nd edition
Denise B. Lacher, Todd Nichols and Joanne C. May
ISBN 978 1 84905 869 8

New Families, Old Scripts
A Guide to the Language of Trauma and Attachment in Adoptive Families
Caroline Archer and Christine Gordon
ISBN 978 1 84310 258 8

Big Steps for Little People

Parenting Your Adopted Child

Celia Foster

Forewords by David Howe and Daniel A. Hughes

Jessica Kingsley *Publishers*
London and Philadelphia

First published in 2008
by Jessica Kingsley Publishers
116 Pentonville Road
London N1 9JB, UK
and
400 Market Street, Suite 400
Philadelphia, PA 19106, USA

www.jkp.com

Library of Congress Cataloging in Publication Data

Foster, Celia, 1956-
Big steps for little people : parenting your adopted child / Celia Foster ; forewords by David Howe and Daniel A. Hughes.
p. cm.
ISBN 978-1-84985-701-7 (pb : alk. paper) 1. Adopted children. 2. Parenting. 3. Adoptive parents. 4. Adoption--Psychological aspects. I. Title.
HV875.F675 2008
649'.145--dc22
2007038856

British Library Cataloguing in Publication Data

A CIP catalogue record for this book is available from the British Library

ISBN 978 1 84985 701 7

Printed and bound in Great Britain

For Luke and Adam

Acknowledgements

I wish to thank my mum, Glynis, Colin, and my dear friend Eileen for their help and encouragement in writing this book, and to Joy – a special thank you as I don't know where we would be without you. I also thank David Howe in the UK and Dan Hughes in the USA for writing their individual forewords.

I thank my friends, my rocks: Lorraine, Anne, Martine, Pat, Tina, Neil and their families for being there for me at the time when I needed you most. I thank all the leaders, assistants and participants of the courses I attended for their willingness to share their innermost thoughts and for the impact that that unselfish sharing has had on my life.

In writing this book I find myself confronted by whom to accredit what to. I have attended so many courses over the years and read so many books that there have been a lot of overlaps in the information covered, so much so that I find it impossible to say who taught me what or indeed who planted the seed of thought which I then went on to develop. I therefore decided to write this book from memory and my interpretation of what I learned along the way. So if I have repeated anything verbatim, I apologize. Please take that as a huge compliment in that you taught me so well. For these people to get the recognition they deserve, I have included a list of the course leaders and the courses I attended in the Appendix at the back of the book.

I thank Chris for his patience, understanding and the huge amount of support and love he has lavished on me throughout the years, and also for his input and help with this book. I really couldn't have done it without you.

Last I thank my darling boys, Luke and Adam, for being who they are, completing my life and teaching me so much about themselves, myself and life in general. All the artwork in this book was produced by the Foster family 'Art Department'.

Contents

Foreword

Adoption, involving issues of loss, family life, identity, and growth and development, has spawned a great deal of reflective literature, much of it autobiographical. Over the last 10 or 20 years, many books have been published on the adoption experience. Some have been by women who have had a child adopted. Others have been written by adopted people describing their experiences of being adopted. And the most recent trend has seen a spate of books about adoption 'reunions' – describing what happens when an adult adopted child searches for, finds and has a reunion with their birth mother, and less commonly birth father. But surprisingly under-represented in the adoption genre are books written by adopted parents. This is understandable, but given the life-changing nature of adoption for all concerned, this is perhaps a pity. Every year, across the world, tens of thousands of people contemplate whether or not to adopt a child. The adoption professionals do their best as they try to get across the reality of adoption but nothing beats the vitality and immediacy of the lived experience described by adopters themselves.

So it is with delight that I welcome the appearance of Celia Foster's book, *Big Steps for Little People: Parenting Your Adopted Child.* It is not so much the story of adopting two young boys, although the reader gets a strong feel of family life *chez* Foster, but more about how Celia and her husband, Chris, faced and dealt with the challenge and joy of parenting two brothers who arrived with so many needs. Typical of many children adopted today, the boys suffered neglect and emotional harm before they were finally placed, aged seven and nearly six, respectively. And from that point on, life would never be the same again for Celia and Chris. The ways in which things changed is described with unflinching clarity. Celia manages to get across with great honesty and humour what family life has been like with Luke and Adam. However, her main purpose is to write a 'what to do' (or more accurately 'what we did') book for the thousands of adoptive parents striving to meet the needs of children whose early lives have been blighted by pain and hurt and fear. Celia pulls no punches. It can be hard, exhausting and sometimes bewildering living with children who arrive with their defences built high, their thoughts confused, and their feelings all over the place. But each little success, each step forward, no matter how small, brings such pleasure to parents and child alike that the reader feels both uplifted and inspired.

In describing what she did when faced with fights, lies, tears, sadness, anxiety, aggression, withdrawal, confused loyalties, eating problems, school concerns, love and affection Celia fashions an extraordinary range of responses, strategies and techniques. She mixes ideas from a wide range of sources but makes them her own, tailor-made to meet the needs and demands of the two brothers. There is much fun along the way. She is the first to acknowledge that some might disagree with some of the things she did, while others might have preferred to tackle problems differently. The point, though, is to encourage adoptive parents to hang in there, to think creatively, to seek support whenever the going gets tough, and to be flexible.

Underpinning this therapeutic creativity and the love the parents and children begin to feel for each other is a tremendous willingness on the part of Celia and Chris to try to understand what the world must feel like and look like from Luke and Adam's point of view, given their terrible beginnings. Out of this empathy flows compassion and sensitivity, understanding and patience. Time and again they have to draw on these reserves when they are faced with set-backs and feelings of helplessness. Two steps forward and one step back is how Celia describes it, but the overall direction is onwards and upwards and by the time we meet the brothers today, seven years later and on the cusp of puberty, the boys have made remarkable progress. She knows that adolescence will throw up new challenges. She knows the dangers of complacency. The key lies in maintaining the empathy, respect and above all the belief that she has in her children. The brothers sense this and they respond.

I am sure that all those involved in the adoption of children, old hands and new, will be stimulated and encouraged by this infectious read.

Dr David Howe
University of East Anglia, Norwich, UK

Foreword

As a therapist, I am continuously looking in two directions for knowledge that will help me to provide treatment for children who have experienced trauma and attachment disorganization. I look to the 'findings' of theorists and researchers of trauma, attachment, and child development on the one hand and to the 'findings' of the foster and adoptive parents of these children on the other. Celia Foster has provided us with loads of knowledge from a parent who was – and is – living day to day where such understanding develops.

Ms Foster's work integrates knowledge about both the 'fire fighting' and the 'underlying issues' which need to be present if the interventions are to be helpful and lasting. She and her husband constantly work to 'figure out' the meaning of their children's behaviours, and then have found many ingenious ways of helping their children to develop an awareness of their thoughts, feelings, and behaviours, and ultimately 'Who am I?' They have found ways to do this without shaming their children – to help their children to experience themselves as being 'normal' given the early environment in which they learned how to live and survive. They help their children to discover both their strengths and their vulnerabilities and to use this awareness in guiding their future development.

This work is a treasure for foster and adoptive parents and for the professionals who work to assist them. Many jewels, such as the 'loving step', the meters for measuring safety, feelings, effort, etc., 'dumping sessions', and the 'loving cup' are sprinkled throughout this book and are likely to impact positively how many parents are able to care for their children. Ms Foster shares with us that raising her two boys has fulfilled one of her biggest wishes to 'make a difference in the world'. Writing this book will,

I believe, also make a difference in the lives of many other foster and adoptive families. I am sure that they will thank her, just as I have done.

Dr Daniel A. Hughes
Clinical psychologist, consultant, trainer and author
Pennsylvania, USA

Preface

I first saw Chris as two of my work colleagues walked across the foyer of the company that I worked in. I went unnoticed as I was making myself a cup of coffee in the staff kitchen. What struck me about Chris that day was that even though he had been terribly burnt in some kind of accident, he appeared full of confidence as he and my two colleagues laughed together. I remember thinking to myself, 'Wow, that man has guts!' He also possessed what I can only describe as an 'extra sparkle', a 'twinkle in his eyes', an 'air of mischief', as though he was somehow more alive than the other two.

A few weeks later I met him again as we all congregated in the bar after a company conference. We found ourselves in the same circle of people and our eyes met as we laughed at a joke. I quickly learned he had the same job as me and worked in a different branch. My first instinct was true – he did have guts, and before the end of the evening he had not only asked me out, but had somehow gained my agreement to go, even though I had vowed to myself that I wasn't going on any more dates unless it was with 'Mr Right'.

Shortly after this I had a small accident. I managed to break my ankle as I opened a heavy door to a company I was visiting and fell off a step. The upshot of this was that I was unable to work for a few months as my job entailed me travelling all over London to visit clients. Chris was brilliant. He kept arriving at my flat with bags of food. Although I know that food is supposed to be the way to a man's heart, I learned in this period of recuperation that it was the way to my heart too. As I was then living on the fifth floor of a block of flats with a very temperamental lift, he soon became my knight in shining armour.

I think what really worked for us and our relationship was that we shared the same passion for life. We both had incredibly positive outlooks gleaned from our interest and involvement in personal development work, and very early on in our relationship we promised each other that we would always be honest with each other and that if either of us decided we wanted to see someone else, then we would call what we had a day. I enjoyed his persistence and greatly admired his courage in that every day he went out and faced the world, when many people with the same injuries would have been far more reluctant to face the stares and comments that he received in the course of his day. His burns were the result of his nightclothes catching fire at the age of four. He spent the following few years in and out of hospital, having countless operations and plastic surgery and then, due to the amount of medication he was on, he had to go to a special school.

He grew up knowing that it didn't matter how bad his injuries were, he had parents and friends who loved him and kept him strong and also he could clearly see, because of the other children he mixed with, that there were a lot of people in a far worse condition than him. In fact he was one of the lucky ones; he had survived. Having had these burns at such an early age, I think there was also an element of this being the norm for him as he grew up knowing nothing else. Had he had the same accident as an adult I think that perhaps the shock of the accident, coupled with the psychological scars, might have been very difficult to cope with. I found that the more I was with him, the less I noticed the scars and the more I came to know and appreciate the man underneath.

One day he arrived with another bag, full of shirts. He announced that he was fed up of travelling across London from his home to mine and he was moving in. Just like that, and as I relate this tale to anyone who asks how we met, I always add: '...and I have never managed to get rid of him since!' After a few months we moved over to his side of London where he was born and grew up. His mum, a widow, was living there, as were a lot of the friends he grew up with. As I had no real attachment to the area I was living in, it seemed the obvious thing to do and there we stayed in our cozy little flat.

After we had been there 5 years, it became apparent that my mum was struggling to cope and look after herself. My father died a few months after I met Chris and Mum was now on one of those never-ending waiting lists for a hip operation. So the three of us decided that we would live together until she felt she could cope on her own again. (This turned out to be about four years later.) We got in our car, headed out of London and kept on driving until we found a place where we could afford to buy a house large enough to let Mum have her own rooms on the ground floor. Chris, now in a different career and earning good money at this time, continued to work in London, whilst I had just been made redundant and was in the fortunate position of being able to take some time out from work whilst I got used to looking after Mum and keeping what seemed to us, after our tiny flat, an enormous house and garden.

About a year later Chris raised the subject of adoption. We had been together for about seven years at this stage, and despite lots of practice I had failed to get pregnant. As I was now 41, as we had already dismissed the idea of IVF treatment, and since neither of us could imagine growing old without children in our lives, we agreed that we would look into adoption. Chris rang social services the next day and made an appointment for a social worker to visit us. I suppose that at this point we had a rose tinted view of adopting the perfect baby and then perhaps having another one a couple of years later. However, when we learned that most adopters are only interested in taking babies and that many children taken into care have to remain in the system as there aren't enough people wanting to take on older children, our view began to change and at this point we were quite prepared to take a family of four or five.

We were then assigned a link worker by social services who taught us all about the process of adoption, helped us with the paper work, and over a period of nine months conducted an assessment for our suitability to adopt. She suggested that whilst we were waiting we should also be assessed to do respite care which means looking after foster children in order to give their carers a break. Respite care could be anything from a couple of hours to a couple of weeks, as the foster parent had a night out, got over an illness or had a holiday. The respite care assessment was a much shorter process and helped us decide what age and how many children we wanted to adopt and also helped me to get used to looking after children. What I found was that I loved having the babies, was not so good with the toddlers (perhaps because they kept running round and needed watching constantly, or perhaps it was because they kept wanting to watch the same DVDs all the time) and to my surprise I thoroughly enjoyed having the older children. Talking this through with Chris we eventually decided that we would like to have two boys over the age of four, preferably brothers, whom we could have at the same time. The more we thought about it, the more we looked forward to helping them overcome the baggage and trauma that they would have incurred as a result of being taken into care.

We (including my mum) started attending training sessions to help prepare us for having children. Chris and I also decided to get married as we were advised that the panel who would review our assessment would view this favourably. We felt that the more stable our relationship was and appeared to be, the better it would be for the children. Incidentally, having done this we felt that our relationship moved to another level and that not only were we now totally committed to each other, but that by getting married we had taken a huge step towards being responsible for the children whom we would adopt. This in turn strengthened our commitment to our future children as we vowed that we would do whatever was necessary to make sure that we didn't end up being just another bit of baggage to put in their very heavy sacks. In short we vowed not to let them down.

Having passed the assessment for adoption, we then had to wait another excruciatingly long nine months before our link worker found the right two boys for us. We read their very brief file, decided to go ahead and were then given their photos, which we immediately put on the mantelpiece and kept staring at. Arrangements went ahead for us to meet the children, but we were then hit by an unexpected blow: we were advised that their birth mother was contesting the adoption and wanted to have them back. Our link worker suggested (which must have been extremely hard for her) that we might want to give up on these children at this point and find some others, but Chris and I reasoned that we had to follow through with these children as they were already expecting to meet their new 'forever' mum and dad. We also learned that their foster parents were keen to take a break from fostering and so the thought that the children might be moved to another foster home if we didn't follow through gave weight to our decision. It was therefore agreed that this was the way forward. We met the children and after a short introductory period they moved in.

I won't enter into all the complications and challenges we faced with the children at this point as the purpose of this introduction is to give you a little background information about Chris, myself and the children. Even though we would dearly love you to think of us as 'super heroes', the reality is that we are just two regular down-to-earth types, with incredibly positive outlooks, facing all the normal challenges of everyday life, who simply refused to give up. At one point the going got incredibly tough; Chris was finding it necessary to stay in accommodation close to his office a lot, due to the ridiculous hours he was having to work. At the same time he was finding it difficult to concentrate whilst he knew that I was struggling with the demanding behaviour the children were displaying and the added pressure I was under for us to allow the children's birth mum to have more contact (even though the children couldn't handle any contact, fell to pieces every time they saw her, and we were left to sort them out). All of this eventually came to a head and Chris had to give up working in London so that he could be at home more and share the burden.

We then entered into a terrible period as he struggled to find suitable work locally and our concerns over money grew, until we were faced with no alternative but to sell up and move closer to London (into a far more humble abode) where the work is. This was all set against the background of having two adorable, though terribly naughty and disturbed, boys living with us, who were calling us Mum and Dad, and all we wanted to do was love them to bits, which was incredibly hard as we didn't know if they were going to stay with us.

Before I go on to talk about the children, I am sure you will understand it has been necessary for me to change the names of all people mentioned in the book, in order to protect their identity. I will also point out that I did endeavour to be politically correct throughout this book and use 'he/she' wherever relevant. However, in practice I found this became cumbersome, especially with the exercises, so I talk about 'he' when relating to my own boys and 'she' at all other times to make for easy reading and to include anyone bringing up girls. In a similar vein I have used 'child' to represent child/children for those of you, who like us, are mad enough to take on more than one child at a time!

Luke was five when he was taken into care and seven and a half when he came to us. Though a bit on the small side, he was and still is an extremely good looking boy, with the kind of face that lights up a room as soon as he walks in, with his lovely smile and a bright twinkle in his eyes. He is definitely one of life's charmers, both with his looks and his personality, or at least the part of him that he chooses to show outsiders. To most people, he appeared a very polite, bright, kind and helpful little boy. It was only when they got to know him better that it was clear that there was actually something not quite right as he seemed overfamiliar, inconsistent, extremely boisterous and perhaps a bit too cocky. He tried to parent Adam and boss us. He was suspicious of everything and everyone and wanted to be involved in our every conversation. He lacked self-confidence and had no humour. He loved to be the centre of attention, and despite his odd and often inappropriate behaviour, he wore his heart on his sleeve, making him a very lovable kid.

Adam was three when he went into care and nearly six when he came to us. Tiny for his age, with a squint and glasses for his bad eyesight, he was also attractive and really cute and has never been afraid to use it! To all who met him, he came across as a very shy, polite, happy and well behaved little boy. He seemed genuinely thrilled to have a new mum and dad and loved to get our approval. On the surface he danced and skipped around the house, which we took as contentedness and happiness, only to realize later that he was living in a kind of fantasy land and that underneath he was a very closed and scared little boy. His issues were hard to read and detect. He seemed completely dominated by Luke and led by whatever mood he happened to be in.

Although on a day-to-day basis Adam's behaviour seemed great in comparison to Luke's, we did have a concern that the 'quiet one' is often the more difficult or troubled. We later found out that he too needed quite a lot of corrective input from us and although he had dealt with his trauma in a different, perhaps more efficient, way to Luke, we felt it was really important that he too went through all the processes described in this book. What we did find with him was that perhaps he was too young to understand everything that we were saying first time round, or at least wasn't ready, so he didn't really start to digest it all until he was nearly nine.

Last I need to introduce you to two more fictitious names: Linda and Tony, the children's birth parents. At first when talking to the boys about them, we called them 'your mum' or 'your dad', or 'your birth mum' or 'your birth dad'. As they called us Mum and Dad from the moment we met them, it all seemed rather silly, not to mention confusing. When things started to go wrong with the contact they had with them and we started doing exercises with the children, we discussed how awkward it was becoming to have two mums and two dads. Asking the children what they wanted to do, they decided that they wanted to call their birth parents by their Christian names as we were the mum and dad whom they saw each day.

Introduction

It is not my aim in writing this book to give you a detailed account of the adoption process or our children's former lives, nor is it my intention to give you a blow-by-blow version or diary of everything that happened when they moved in with us. I will, however, share with you snippets of information where relevant to the points that I want to make and would like to emphasize that I do so with the boys' full knowledge and consent. They have readily allowed me to repeat many of the steps, exercises and techniques we have used in this book, which serve both as a reminder for them as they are older now and perhaps enable them to 'get' the message at a deeper level. This has also helped us ensure that we had remembered the original words we used and that they made sense. In turn the boys were able to remind me of techniques I had forgotten about and to tell me what they had liked about doing this work and the effect that it had on them. They really like the idea that, having been helped themselves, we might now as a family be able to help other children through this book.

The ideas for this book stem from our passion to learn everything we can about human behaviour, a subject that Chris and I have both been involved with and intrigued by for the past 18 years. We are particularly interested in the questions of why we as human beings behave the way we do and why one person will react to something one way, whilst another will react to the same thing in a completely different way; how our minds are like the most powerful computers; how as human beings we are capable of the most amazing things, yet we only seem to use a small portion of our brain's capacity, and how our minds can be reprogrammed with new 'software' to overcome the most painful of memories and deep-routed conditioning. In raising the boys we have used the techniques which we studied over the years, or at least our interpretation of them. Many we have adapted to suit their needs and many we have made up ourselves. What we have become particularly good at is not giving up. If one thing doesn't work, we simply devise another way and if that doesn't work, we find yet another way to get through to them.

We first thought of writing a book soon after the boys moved in and we discovered the full extent of the pain and trauma they had suffered whilst in their birth home, the consequent damage and effect that had on them, the challenges they faced, and the added pressures incurred as they were taken into care. The true extent of the damage they incurred wasn't apparent and didn't surface until they were faced with settling into their 'for ever home'. So whilst they were quite well behaved in their foster homes (we were told that Luke might need 'taking down a peg or two', but that was the only concern), when they moved in with us, it was quite a different story.

At that time there were many books which explained why traumatized children behave the way they do, but no books about what to do. Having attended many courses (many courtesy of social services) desperately trying to find answers to our questions, it became blatantly apparent that most of the other participants felt exactly the same. At each course we attended we sat on the edge of our seats waiting for the 'how to' part of the course, only to be bitterly disappointed with just a few basic tips or, worse than that, none at all. I am not, of course, recommending that you boycott such courses. It is very useful to understand on these kinds of courses why and where the behaviours of adopted children come from. It is also extremely comforting to mix with people who are in a similar boat. We realized that we were not alone in facing these challenges and if nothing else the courses served to show that we were already on the right track. In the early days we decided to attend every course with a completely open mind and were extremely happy if either of us went away with even one thing that might help, even if we had learned it from another participant rather than the trainers.

The real decision to write this book came after I was asked to speak at a post-adoption support group meeting about raising the self-esteem of adopted children. A second speaker was to talk about raising the self-esteem of the adoptive mother (mother, because there were no stay-at-home fathers in our group and it was, in our experience, the parent at home/main carer who bore the brunt of the children's behaviour). Ever since then the question of how we raise the self-esteem of adopted children has stuck with me, and the more I thought about it, the more I realized how difficult it was to talk about such a vast subject for such a short time, in that so *many* factors contributed to raising our children's self-esteem.

We are not, of course, experts with every child. We are not even experts with our own children although we have come an extremely long way in understanding their issues and in overcoming many of them. Are they perfect? Yes. We firmly believe that all children are perfect, just as they are. Is our children's behaviour perfect? No, but do any of us truly behave perfectly all of the time and what is perfect anyway? Have they improved? Yes, massively. Was adopting them what we expected? No. If we knew back then what we know now, would we still have adopted them? Yes, definitely. Was it worth it? Yes, absolutely. The whole experience has far exceeded all our expectations. We completely love our children to bits. Yes, there were times when the going was tough and we didn't know what to do, but overall the benefits of having faced and met those challenges are enormous, both to the boys and ourselves, and the satisfaction of seeing the smiles on their faces whilst they dance around the house shouting, 'I'm free!' and 'I love myself!' has touched and moved us at the very deepest level.

In writing this book I can only tell you about the challenges we faced with our own children and how we chose to deal with and overcome them. Indeed, we know of other couples with very different views on how to raise adopted children, who have been equally successful. Your child may be very different from our two, or you may find similarities. It is my hope that a lot of what I write can be adapted to suit your child. Please be aware, though, that I am not trying to tell you what you *should* do. I would merely like to share with you what worked for us. So please read this book with an open mind. Try on what I am saying and, if it fits, go ahead and use it, or adapt it to suit your needs, and if it doesn't fit perhaps it might at least encourage you to approach your child's challenges differently.

So who will this book benefit? It is my hope that it will help anyone who is considering or has already adopted an older child. I also hope that it may be of interest to all adoptive parents as I have heard of many adopted babies who go on to have reactions to their adoptive state later on in life. I would also like to think that social workers and other interested professionals might gain a better understanding of what can happen after adoption, and that foster parents might read the book as they often have to prepare foster children for adoption. How great it would be if some of the ideas in this book were started in the foster home and then continued as the child moves into their adoptive home. This book could also prove useful in raising the self-esteem of a child who was to be returned to his birth parents or family. Having listed all those who will find this book useful, it is my firm belief that we would have used many of the ideas in this book if we had had children naturally.

The biggest challenge in writing this book was not thinking up the ideas. When we got over the shock of the boys moving in, finally stopped doubting our abilities to cope, stopped relying on the 'experts' to advise us and started trusting our own instincts, we found the ideas came thick and fast. The hardest thing in writing the book was deciding which bits were most important and what order to write them in. To me it seemed that everything was important and all needed to be said first! Also, to be completely honest, some of the ideas came to us later rather than sooner, so it was difficult to know whether to write the book as though we did everything right from the start or to write it as and when the solutions came to us. (Our observation here is that it doesn't really matter how old the child is or in what order you present the various processes contained in this book; the important thing is that they do actually do the work).

We have learned a lot of things the hard way, through making mistakes, and whereas 'hindsight' is not really of any use to us, it may well be of use to you, in that you can learn from our mistakes. In the end I decided that it would make easier reading if I attempted to write the book in the order that you might need it. I have therefore endeavoured to arrange the contents in a logical order and suggest you read it all. However, if you are desperate to find ways of handling bad behaviour, you might want to head straight for Chapters 8, 9 and 10, which are about learning to express emotions, handling bad behaviour and control issues.

Having said that, it is our firm belief that 'fire fighting' or handling bad behaviour is all well and good, but in a way it is only papering over the cracks and may only give you a few minutes/hours of peace and quiet. If the underlying issues are faced and dealt with in conjunction with these techniques, the process of healing and repairing the child will happen a whole lot quicker. By addressing these deep-rooted problems head on, we have succeeded in having our children understand their issues, accept them and move on. They are now developing (for the most part) into two well-behaved, socially aware, well adjusted young people, with values, beliefs and integrity of their own. More importantly, they have decided that this is how *they* want and choose to live *their* lives.

For those of you who have taken on a child who for all intents and purposes seems to be totally well adjusted and handling their adoptive state in an efficient way, a word of warning. I have, I'm afraid to report, heard of several children who have managed to 'hold it together' successfully for several years only to fall apart when puberty strikes. For this reason I would urge you to do the appropriate exercises in this book with them anyway. It certainly won't do them any harm, and maybe putting in a bit of time and effort while they are relatively young will prevent the pain incurred by all concerned later.

It is definitely not my intention to put people off the idea of adopting. Yet I honestly believe that it takes a certain 'type' to adopt. Indeed, I believe that by understanding the potential challenge up front, although it may put some people off (which is not always a bad thing given that some adoptions 'break down'), to balance this it may well encourage others to do something that they had hitherto not thought of. Not every child will display the same levels of odd behaviour and require the same amount of input in terms of reparation as our children. Some will require more and some less. I think that if you are determined and enjoy a challenge, you may well feel totally fulfilled and as thrilled as we do to have achieved all that you have and proud that your child overcomes whatever they need to overcome. I never had children naturally, yet these two children feel so 'right' to me. They have completed my life, I love them dearly and I know that if necessary I would (just as I assume any natural parent would do) die to save them.

I make no excuse for the style of writing or the language that I have used in this book. The style and language will aid you in learning and digesting the concepts. Although you will read a little about the use of effective language later, to explain it fully would be a book on its own. I have therefore included throughout the book the language that we find effective and in everyday use in our house in the hope that you will pick it up for yourselves. I would also add that I have explained fully the key methods, concepts and distinctions featured in this book to the children, in this same language. The best way we have found to do this is to state the concept as it is and then find more age-appropriate words to explain it fully, then to repeat the original explanation. By introducing them to words that they were probably hitherto unfamiliar with makes them stand out for the child and take on significant meaning when used in day-to-day conversations.

I make no apology for the length of time it took us to get around to writing this book. I say 'us' as Chris had a considerable input in discussing and formulating ideas both for the children in our everyday lives and the book and was of course involved in presenting many of our ideas to them. Yes, we could see that there was a huge need for it, but our priorities had to, and still do, lie with sorting our own children out first.

Chapter 1

Being Taken into Care

You are five years old. You are a dirty, smelly, scruffy kid and can't remember the last time you had clean clothes, a bath or a proper meal. Your head still hurts from where you tried to cut your hair and took a big chunk out of your scalp. You are sitting on the floor of your lounge. The carpet is filthy and littered with beer cans and overflowing ashtrays. The walls are still marked with smoke damage, from the fire you started in the electricity box. You can't settle. Your little half-sister is out with her dad and has been gone for ages and surely should be back by now. Fraught with anxiety you rush to the window every other minute, drawing back the curtain straining to see if they are coming. Your three-year-old brother, Adam, is watching television with his nose pressed right up against the screen. You walk over and punch him for no reason at all. He sits there snivelling.

Your tummy is empty. It's gone past the rumbling stage and now aches. You haven't had a single thing to eat all day and it doesn't matter how many times you look in the fridge or open the cupboard doors, there is no food in the house. You think about going out to search next door's bin. Your mum has passed out on the settee from her usual mixture of booze and drugs, but of course you don't realize or understand that. You keep going over to prod her, but she isn't going to wake up, so instead you put a blanket over her to keep her warm. Dad left the family home ages ago, in fact just after your brother Adam was born. You did go and see him once. You sneaked out of the house, crossing the busy roads by yourself, but he sent you home again. Your mum didn't even notice you were missing.

Eventually your sister and Nick, her dad, come back home. She is beaming with delight because she's just had a nice time with her dad. She had plenty of attention and has got food in her belly. He walks over to Linda and tries to wake her, but it doesn't matter how hard he shakes her, she doesn't wake up. He goes into the hall and you hear him on the telephone, but even though you really try, you can't hear what he is saying. Soon there is a loud banging at the door. It is two policemen. You can't stop them. They just walk right in. They are huge and scary, and seem to fill the whole room. They tell you, you can't live with your family or in this house any more and no, you don't have time to think about it, in fact you have no say whatsoever in this matter. You just need to go with them NOW. Come on, no, there's no time to say, 'Goodbye'. There's no time to pack. You've got to go right now. Just like that. Your world has been turned upside down.

* * * * *

Now close your eyes, step into that child's body and really think about it. Picture the scene and really feel, see and hear what he must have seen, heard and felt. Feel his fear, the sense of utter disbelief and the unheard cries of, 'What's happening?' This is what happened to our children. They ran away from the police and tried to hide. They describe being absolutely petrified as they were chased, caught, then bundled into a police car and taken away. Luke described feeling awful as he kicked one of them, an event that haunted him in years to come, which went a long way to help fuel the ideas that he was a 'bad child'. They were only appeased when they were safely in the police canteen and were given a Mars bar each, which, given how hungry they were and their vivid descriptions of their mouths dribbling, must have been the best Mars bar in the world! Yet for two very hungry boys, that wasn't enough.

We didn't have any of this information, when the boys were about to move in. In fact we had very little to go on at all. Chances are that you won't either. It was only much later when the boys started confiding in us, and social services made their files available to us, that we were able to understand the enormity of what had happened to them. So please borrow our scenario, really feel what it's like for a child to be taken from their birth home and placed into care. Of course, every story will be different, but whether the child finds herself in care because her parents are ill, dead or in prison, whether children have suffered from neglect, physical, emotional or sexual abuse, they will all have suffered in some way from their trauma. I remember in one of the very early training sessions I attended, I was asked to imagine someone knocking on my door and telling me that I had to move away from my family, my home and everything that was familiar and dear to me and imagine being placed with a new family, in a different house and a different town. It is horrendous to contemplate even as an adult. Yet for these children it was reality and it doesn't matter where they came from, how awful their lives were, how badly they were parented and how much they needed to be taken into care, they were taken from *their* mother, *their* home and everything that they knew and that was completely normal to them.

Now think about how, having been together all their lives, they are then separated from their half-sister who was taken by her father (and still lives with him) and although together for the first night the two boys were then put into separate foster homes.

You are absolutely petrified. It's the middle of the night. Your tummy is in agony because all you've had to eat all day was a Mars bar. A lady came to the police station to get you and has taken you to a strange house. A woman meets you at the door, she seems nice and smiles at you, but you don't smile back. You don't want the woman to like you or be nice to you because you are 'bad' and you are scared, and all you want is to be back at home with your mum asleep on the settee. That is what you know. That is what you are used to. That is your home. You hang your head in shame. You are feeling very, very bad. The police came to get you and they took you away. They only deal with very bad people. You are to blame for everything that happened. It's your fault, because you put a blanket over your mum encouraging her to sleep.

The new lady takes you into the kitchen and gives you both a sandwich and a glass of milk. It doesn't taste very nice, but given how hungry you are, you wolf it down in case she takes it away from you, which makes your tummy hurt even more. She then takes you both upstairs to a bathroom. She runs a bath and orders you to strip off your clothes. She puts them into a bin bag then ties the top of the bag in a knot. She tells you both to get into the bath. It stinks of a smell that is totally unfamiliar to you. She then takes a scrubbing brush and scrubs away all over your head and body until your skin feels red and raw. When it's Adam's turn to be scrubbed, he starts to snivel and whine. She then dries you and drags a comb through your hair and makes you clean your teeth. She gives you pyjamas to put on and takes you both to a bedroom with bunk beds in it. You understand these. You had a bunk bed once, you used to bounce up and down on it and swing off the bars, until one day it collapsed. You didn't get into trouble though, your mum didn't seem to care, but she never got round to fixing it, so from that day on, you had to sleep on the mattresses on the floor and when you had wrecked Adam's mattress by jumping on it so much, that was thrown into the garden and you both had to share the remaining mattress, which wasn't very nice because Adam used to wet himself every night.

Everything feels wrong. The room is clean and tidy and smells odd. Reluctantly, you get into bed and she turns off the light. The room is dark and shadowy with spooky corners. You lie there listening to the strange noises of the house, trembling because there are monsters under the bed. You hear Adam breathing deeply and know that he has fallen straight to sleep. You toss and turn and because you're not used to having a quilt, get into a fight with it and you struggle to get free as it gets wrapped round your legs. Eventually you fall into a restless sleep.

In the morning you wake up and immediately sit bolt upright, which makes you feel dizzy. You are laying the wrong way round in a strange bed, in a strange room. You remember the events of the previous evening and hope they were all a dream. You hit yourself hard on the head to check if you are really awake. Unfortunately you are.

The lady from the night before comes into the room. She gives you some clothes to put on. They don't fit very well and they have the same odd smell as the pyjamas she gave you last night. She takes you down to her kitchen and gives you cereal, which you bolt down in two seconds flat, whilst Adam sucks on every little bit, making it last for ages. You look round sheepishly wishing you had the guts to ask for some more.

The doorbell goes. It's the lady who came to get you from the police station last night. She now takes you with her to another house, where another lady lives. To your utter dismay, she leaves your brother there, and takes you to yet another house. You are mortified. Your heart is racing. You can't believe what is happening to you; you have never been so scared in your whole life.

As the lady shows you round the house, the penny begins to drop. You are expected to stay here now. Separated from your mum, brother and sister, this is to be your home. She shows you a bedroom, which is to be yours. She gives you clothes to wear that don't belong to you. You hate it here. You think you will never get used to it. Everything is so different. There is so much to get used to, but you decide that you must try really hard and behave. You must make them like you, because you can't imagine what will happen to you if they don't. But it's hard. They expect so much of you.

After a lifetime of eating scraps, usually from the floor or bin, you are now expected to sit at a table, use a knife and fork, eat a full and hot meal, and make polite conversation. You now have to sleep in a proper bed with clean sheets, when all you've ever known since you broke your bunk bed is a damp, urine-stained mattress on the floor, which you had to share with your brother. They seem to expect you to be able to cope with their way of doing things and all their routines and all the time you are screaming inside, 'Where's my mum? Where are my brother and sister? What's happening?' And your new foster parents want to get to know you. They want you to look them in the eye, but you know that if you do that, they will see what you are really like, they'll get to know how 'bad' you are and then they will send you away too.

You've just started to settle into some kind of life. You've been assigned a social worker so some of your questions have been answered, but you hate her because she won't let you go back to your mum and you love her because she manages to persuade your foster mother to let Adam move in with you too. Life starts to get better when he arrives. You are getting used to the routines and like having food, clean clothes and going to school each day. You've seen your mum a couple of times, though you still worry that she's not all right and wonder how she will cope and if she will remember to buy food for herself when you aren't there to remind her and how will she manage without you to lean on and do everything for her. And you still don't understand why you can't go back. Then suddenly, completely out the blue, you are told that you can't stay in this house any more. This surely is more confirmation that you are bad and it doesn't matter what they tell you, you know deep down inside, it's just an excuse. They don't want you any more either because you are so very bad.

Now you are in a different foster home and you've got to get used to another set of people, their rules and routines and their house smells funny and their food tastes different from the last house, and this time the monsters live in the wardrobe, the house makes creaking sounds, and you can see faces in the patterns in the curtains at night. You are seeing your mum sometimes, but you still don't understand why you can't go back and live with her. When you see her now she seems much better and you have fun with her and she showers you with presents. Then just when you begin to feel a little bit more settled you are told that you are to be moved yet again and all the feelings of being bad come flooding back again. These people obviously think you are so horrible that they don't want you any more either. Only this time you are told that you are going to be moved to two very odd looking people and now, on top of everything else, you are expected to call them Mum and Dad and you are told that you are going to stay there for ever, which of course means that you are never going home.

So you've got to get used to yet another house with all its dark corners and strange smells, noises, and monsters. You've got to get used to these odd people who seem to think they are your mum and dad, but inside you are screaming, 'I've already got a mum and dad' and you call them 'Mum' and 'Dad', which feels very strange, but that's what you've been told to do. You have to get used to an old woman who calls herself 'Granny', but you've already got two grannies and they are both much younger and this 'granny' can barely walk.

Got the picture? Obviously this is just a very rough sketch of what being taken into care was like for our children. For others it is even worse, with countless moves from pillar to post. Our children were in fact quite lucky, as they had excellent foster homes and their carers were incredibly supportive. It's important to remember that our children had no choice in any of this. They didn't get to pick us. They had no say and if the whole experience of being taken into and living in care wasn't enough torture to endure, all this happened on top of the deprivation, neglect and abuse they suffered whilst with their birth parents.

Chapter 2

Settling In

Bearing in mind the children's troubled beginnings we felt it was important for them to keep their belongings and clothes (even the tatty ones) for as long as they needed to give them a sense of continuity and belonging. We let them put photos of their birth mum, Linda, on their bedside table and even let Luke cuddle up each night with the large red devil that Linda had bought him, even though the thought of having a devil of any type in our house was not easy for us. (She had bought him this because she used to call him 'my little devil', supposedly affectionately!) Even though we were tempted to throw everything out and start again, we realized that the children might see that as us going against Linda, putting her down in some way, trying to dent the image they had of their past. We felt that this was a kind of transition period for them whilst they got used to us and that having some of their former stuff to comfort them would make it a lot easier. We also figured that these items would lose interest for them as they became more attached to us and that, like their clothes, they would grow out of them when they were ready.

We let them pick their rooms and quilt covers and have a say in how they wanted their bedroom furniture arranged. We tried to use their favorite colours in the décor, but in soothing tones, choosing to keep it simple in an attempt not to overwhelm them. We were glad that we had followed this approach, because both rooms were very quickly trashed. We even used the same soap powder their foster parents used hoping that the continuation of smell would help them settle at an unconscious level. We purposely didn't go overboard with the amount of new stuff we gave them, thinking it better to introduce new things gradually, as and when they could handle it. We found it interesting that Luke chose the smallest bedroom (we had expected him to choose the largest) but then worked out that, as with other children who had stayed with us (we did some respite care while we were waiting for the boys to be placed), it was because this was where he would feel safest. We didn't make a fuss. We simply told him that when he felt ready he might want to move into the larger room, as he would have more room to play. Adam seemed quite content in the third bedroom, which was warm and cozy. He immediately made it his own, by recreating the smells he was familiar with, in the form of bedwetting each night!

We decided not to introduce the boys to too many of their new family and our friends all at once as we didn't want to overwhelm them. We chose simply to close the door and spend a lot of time together getting to know each other, start the process of bonding and attachment and concentrate on making ourselves strong as a family unit. For the same reasons we held back on treats and outings, feeling that there would be plenty of time for that in the future, but for now it was just important to find out what being in our family was going to be like. We quickly introduced the boys to the ground rules of the house, explaining that as and if it became necessary, we would add new ones or adapt the ones we'd made.

Ground rules

- You must wait for us when you wake up in the mornings before going downstairs. Please feel free to knock on our door when you wake.
- Only grown-ups are allowed to answer the doorbell or telephone.
- If you feel hungry or want a drink, please ask.
- Granny would prefer it if you didn't play in her rooms unless invited.
- If Granny wants you to get something, please do so, as she is often in a lot of pain and can't walk very well.
- You may play in the back garden, but not in the front.
- If you want something or are not sure, please ask.

- You must ask if it's all right to watch television.
- Please respect Mum, Dad and Granny.

Obviously those reading this book will make their own ground rules to suit their needs. It is, of course, important to remember at this stage not to be fazed. You don't necessarily know what to expect right now, but one thing for sure is that you will have a far better idea than your child, and whatever you provide (in most cases) will be better than where they originally came from. Before our children moved in with us, we had very real concerns that they would compare us and our house with the beautiful farm that they had been lucky enough to live on in their last foster home. The reality, though, was that they made no comparisons at all between them and us, or their house and ours. The only comparisons made were between our home and their birth home. We received many comments in those early days about all the magnificent things that they had owned and been parted from. Obviously those were attempts to have us shower them with lots of things they had never had. Luke, in particular, defended his birth mother and his old way of life with a vengeance, always comparing me to her and delighting if he thought I'd made a mistake with something. We found it useful to use statements like, 'In this house we do it this way' and 'In our family we like to...'.

Ground rules for adults

Chris, Mum and I had already talked long and hard about the way we wanted to parent the children and how we wanted to bring them up. We had made the following ground rules for the three of us:

- We would always sing off the same hymn sheet and check if we were told that one of the others had said something was okay to do.
- We would never undermine the others' authority.
- We would stick with whatever decision the other had made, even when ridiculous and made in the heat of the moment (we did a lot of that in the early days).
- We would always support and respect each other.
- We would always put on a united front.

- We would not argue in front of the children.
- We would demonstrate our love for each other and show our affection openly, attempting to show the boys that we were not about to split up as their birth parents had and that this is what a healthy relationship looks like.
- We agreed with Granny that Chris and I were the bosses (over the children) in the children's eyes and it would be good if she could refer them back to us as often as possible, but of course if they were being naughty in our absence, she would intervene.

Putting on a united front like this proved invaluable, as Luke often tried to test our relationship by playing one of us off against the other and would dearly have loved to split us, but we stood firm and eventually he began to realize that we had a very strong relationship and that, if one of us said no, we both meant no. He was amazed that even without the two of us conferring we often gave exactly the same answer to the same question and soon learned that he was not going to win in his attempts to divide us. We were and still are solid.

School

We talked to the headmistress of the school and arranged for the boys to do a few half days until they felt ready to go full time. Many people say that once their children have started school full time, they collect them at lunchtime as a way of breaking them in slowly. In hindsight we see that they might possibly have benefited from a short period of doing this. At the time, however, we felt it important for them to get used to being at school through lunch as this is when the bonding process with other children really starts.

Some people have told me that they chose not to tell the school that their children were adopted. Of course that is up to you to decide. We reasoned that it might be better to tell the school as we thought they might be able to help us, as they were perhaps used to dealing with adopted children and children in care. We also felt it was important for the school to know the facts so that if our children were to misbehave they would understand that this wasn't as a result of anything happening in their home now and that we were supporting them to be the very best that they could be. As time went on, we were able to advise the school when the children were having contact with their birth parents and when they were having therapy, in order that the school were aware of the extra pressures they were under, to let the school know how the children were coping and how we would like the school to handle any situations that arose as a consequence of either of these.

We decided that we wanted the children to be known by our surname right from the start. Our reasoning was that, when it became necessary for the boys to change their name when/if they were adopted, it would save them having to explain that away, as they might not be able to handle the kind of comments they might receive from other children. With this in mind, we strongly recommended that they themselves didn't tell anyone, especially other children, that they were being adopted as most children don't know what adoption is and can be pretty nasty about anything that they don't understand or anything that makes another child different. Here we pointed out to them that although a child might be 'your best friend', you don't actually know how that child will respond to this kind of information and once you have told someone and your 'story' is potentially out, you can never take it back again.

We taught them lots of one-liners at this point in case they were teased about Chris's face, so that if anyone said anything along the lines of, 'Your dad's got a scarred face', they could shoot straight back at them with, 'Yes he has and he's really great!' They very quickly learned that if they appeared unbothered by what other children say, they would soon lose interest and stop saying things and, just as with bullying, the aggressor only persists if the target shows signs of weakness and is affected by the torments.

We gave the children transitional objects to keep with them at all times to remind them that we were their new parents, that we loved them, and that they belonged with us in their new family. The purpose of this is to keep the child focused and remind them that they are all right and safe now, if their minds start to drift while they are away from you. I put little notes for them to find in their lunch boxes. We gave them one of those little laminated cards that you can buy with verses and words of wisdom on, in this case about being our son, to keep in their pockets. Then we had a photo of us as a family made into a key ring, which they clipped onto their pencil cases. Likewise when Chris had to go away on business he asked them each to look after an inexpensive pen of his while he was away and told them he would need it back when he returned. This served as a reminder that he would be coming back. He also made taped messages of his voice and of course rang them each day.

I made a point of asking them what they had done each day, really took an interest, and frequently let them see me talk to their teachers. I made sure that I was always early to pick them up because I knew that as soon as they saw other parents arriving in the playground, they would start to get anxious. Together we invented a secret password (which we gave to the school) to be used in case of emergencies, which would be given to whoever I got to pick them up. I told them that under no circumstance were they ever to go with anyone else other than Chris, Granny, or myself unless the teacher told them someone was coming and they knew the password.

Inevitably it wasn't long before Luke's teacher beckoned me in to speak with her. I came to dread those moments, as I could sense that all the other parents knew she wanted to speak to me because my child had been naughty. With a sense of foreboding I always asked, 'What's he done now?' ('He' being Luke; Adam was never in trouble at school, or at least not until he was much older and that was more for talking in class when he eventually found his voice than anything serious.) I did, however, always make a point of getting Luke's version first, so as to let him know that I thought what he had to say was more important. Physically I stood next to him and held his hand whilst he was being remonstrated in the hope that he would understand I was on his side. When I spoke to him I asked what he thought *we* could do in helping him find a solution or better strategy to deal with what had occurred.

Initial promises

On their second day we sat them down and told them that we empathized with them and their situation, that although we could only *guess* at how scary it must have been for them to be taken away from their birth mum, we were trying very hard to think about how difficult it was for them. We also acknowledged how hard it must have been moving from foster home to foster home, having to get used to living with different people and their way of life. We explained that we understood that they already had a (birth) mum and dad and it must seem very odd for them that they now had a new mum and dad as well. We told them we appreciated how hard it must be to have to settle into yet another house, with new people, new smells, new food, new routines, etc. and that we were going to do everything we could think of to make it as easy as possible for them. Most importantly we told them that we were sure everything was going to work out all right. We assured them that the feelings that they were having right now were completely normal and that we were sure that if the same things had happened to us, then we would feel the same way too. On a piece of paper we wrote the following promises:

- There is nothing to fear in this house.
- We will always keep you safe.
- Nothing nasty will happen to you now.
- We will always do our best for you.
- You will always have enough food and drink.
- You are always going to be warm.
- You will always have electricity.
- You will always have clothes.
- We are your friends.
- We hope that one day you will be able to trust us.

We then signed it and stuck it on one of the kitchen cupboard doors for all to see. Every few days we would refer back to it as a way of reminding them that we were keeping our word.

We discovered that by putting posters, schedules, charts, targets, etc. on cupboard doors, walls and notice boards, they were somehow more acceptable, possibly because the children didn't have to keep making eye contact with us and they didn't feel as though they were being lectured, or possibly because they just seemed more official. The children were also reminded that no one else had ever taken this much interest in them before, and indeed they appeared quite pleased and surprised after our initial talk to find that we were prepared to go to such lengths. Our children have always responded well to this kind of communication and even now we find this to be effective.

Some people talk of a glorious 'honeymoon period', when the children arrive and are on their best behaviour in an attempt to impress and everyone has time to get to know each other. This was not so in our case, or if we did have a 'honeymoon period' it lasted for only a day or two. It felt to us as if the boys walked in the house, looked at us, looked around, then said to themselves, 'This will do' and then let rip! We felt as though we were thrown in at the deep end right from the start. Some issues like Adam's bedwetting we decided virtually to ignore; we just quietly gave him a shower or bath each morning and changed his sheets, assuring him that he would grow out of it. With Adam's whining we simply said, 'There's no need for that', and with Luke's terrible night tremors, we religiously woke him, reassured him and settled him again, often several times a night. Other matters became more pressing and needed urgent attention.

Food issues, rules and solutions

Neither boy would eat properly. Luke usually wanted nothing other than best meat, vegetables and potatoes – which there had been in abundance in their last foster home on the farm, cereal or dried bread – which perhaps reminded him of former times. This proved difficult for us as we don't eat that much meat. Anything else we gave him he would refuse to eat and once even spat his food out all over us and the table. Sometimes he would seem to like other foods, only to dislike them the next time they were presented and having no memory of having liked them before. He usually gulped his food noisily, perhaps in the fear that it would disappear or perhaps because that was the only way he knew how to eat. We often used to find that when he got home from school he would rush to the fridge, throw the door open and take great delight to find it full of food. Conversely when he did this and found it nearly empty he would start to get extremely anxious and I had to tell him that I had enough food in for dinner that night and breakfast the next morning, tell him what we were having, and assure him that I would be going shopping the next day. Other times I'd admit that the fridge was looking a bit empty, but show him what I'd got in the cupboards and deep freeze and reassure him that I was not the type of person who ever ran out of food.

Adam was incredibly frail. His skin was so thin you could almost see through it. So his eating habits were of even more concern to us. He seemed only to like macaroni with tomato sauce, pizza and cereal. Despite being nearly six, some of the clothes he arrived with were for a two to three-year-old. His poor eating habits featured in every report (that we later got to see) from every person who had been responsible for his care right back to when he was with his birth mum. He would eat just tiny amounts, taking forever to chew and swallow his food. He stored food in his cheeks like a hamster and it would still be there hours after he had left the table. Sometimes he would put too much in his mouth at once and then, before he had chewed and swallowed, add more. Often he would retch. At other times he would sit there pretending to chew his food, while all the time we could see that it was still in his cheek. He obviously feared that he might not get any more food and was thus determined to make it last as long as possible.

Watching Adam eat was painfully boring, incredibly frustrating and unpleasant. We tried everything under the sun to improve his eating habits, from feeding him ourselves, to breaking down the eating process, teaching him how to do each step. When that didn't work we tried ignoring him. We tried starting his meal before everyone else, letting him eat separately from everyone else, leaving him at the table when everyone else had finished and giving him smaller portions. We tried letting him serve himself, but he'd pile his plate with enough food for two people and only eat a small fraction of what was there, and then in desperation taking his plate away (regardless of the amount he had eaten) when everyone else had finished. This, I am sad to report, actually had the best effect, especially if we coupled this with an early night.

One day the boys' Guardian Ad Litum (an officer of the Court appointed to ensure their wellbeing) came to dinner to observe the children in their new surroundings. To our complete and utter surprise, Adam ate his meal perfectly, finished first, put his knife and fork together and said, 'Thanks Mum. That was absolutely delicious!' We nearly fell off our chairs. Although we hadn't told the boys how important her visit was, it was as if they somehow decided for themselves and they weren't going to do anything that would sway her into thinking that they should be moved again. From that moment on I realized that Adam had been playing games all along; he was perfectly capable of eating normally. He actually enjoyed the amount of attention he was getting by worrying us with his eating habits. He also liked the feelings he got when in desperation we all left the room, as he liked being the 'victim', the one who was left out. Or at least that gave him feelings that he was used to. These feelings reminded him of the past. It was all he had ever known and in a twisted way made him feel secure.

Eat o'meter

It was then that I decided to make a few eating rules and I introduced the eat o'meter:

- You are expected to eat the meal that has been prepared for you. That is what there is.
- If you don't eat your main course there is no pudding and nothing else until the next meal.
- If you don't finish your main course by the time everyone else has finished, your plate will be cleared away. There is no pudding and nothing else until the next meal.
- You cannot leave the table until everyone else has finished (invented for Luke, in an attempt to slow him down).
- If you choose to play with your food we will assume that you have finished and take your plate away.

These rules were then boldly written on paper and stuck on the wall.

The eat o'meter chart was simple: if they ate their meal well they gained a tick and could score up to three ticks for a day. I then staggered the amount of ticks needed over a week, starting with a low target, to coax them into eating, so that for week one they needed to have scored ten points to win a spin on the spin o'meter, whereas by week four, they needed to score a minimum of 19 points. I kept the prizes simple: they could stay up late, choose a game to play, win 50 pence, etc. I advise that you make up the prizes to suit yourself. They need to be simple, easy and must be rewarded quickly to gain full impact.

Eat o'meter

	Breakfast	Lunch	Dinner	Total
Sun	✔	✔		2
	✔		✔	2
Mon		✔	✔	2
	✔	✔		2
Tue		✔	✔	2
	✔			1
Wed	✔			1
	✔	✔	✔	3
Thur	✔		✔	2
		✔		1
Fri	✔			1
		✔	✔	2
Sat	✔	✔	✔	3
	✔	✔	✔	3

Week 1 – score of 10 or more wins a spin __13__
Week 2 – score of 13 or more wins a spin __14__
Week 3 – score of 16 or more wins a spin ______
Week 4 – score of 19 or more wins a spin ______

Spin o'meter

You have won

The judge's decision is final!!

Figure 2.1: Eat o'meter and spin o'meter

I was so concerned about the children's eating habits that I consulted several people about this and was repeatedly advised that I should stick to my guns and not make a rod for my own back by making different meals for everyone and that the children would soon get used to my cooking. A social worker told me that she'd never heard of a child in care starving to death and that they would eat when they wanted to. It made me feel terrible, having to be so tough, but I knew that I had to persevere, as I couldn't let the children use food as a weapon, either to get at me, or to remind themselves of feelings they had in the past.

Sometimes in an attempt to get them to like new foods, I would make a buffet type meal with lots of different dishes, fruits and vegetables to try. I would then leave some of their favourite food on a work top away from the table telling them that when they had participated fully in the food trial, they could eat whatever I'd left on the side. I made this fun by giving them small tasters on cocktail sticks. I even tried blindfolding them. At other times I would give them a tiny plate with three new foods on it and tell them that they could have their real dinner only when they had tried what was on the plate. I later learnt that it takes ten times of presenting a new food to a child before they will accept it and like it.

Their eating habits improved almost immediately. The boys loved the eat o'meter and pronounced that no one had ever made them anything like that before. It wasn't long before they declared me to be 'the best cook and mum in the world!' Though Luke has recently admitted that he used to say he hated my cooking, the truth was that he probably didn't like it because he tried so few foods when he was young and he was scared to try new ones. We kept the eat o'meter going for three or four months until the boys were eating better and only stopped it when they started complaining about the prizes. From time to time they still go back to their old habits, especially Adam, but these days we are a lot tougher or perhaps wiser and are quickly able to bring them back into line. It is amazing how quickly they remember the rules if you have to take their plate away. Please note that we really didn't have to do this more than two or three times and there were always long gaps in between.

Incidentally, as we're talking about food, I decided that I would start as I meant to carry on and made sure that each day they received at least five portions of fruit and vegetables and ate the right amount of protein and other food components. I didn't completely rule out the occasional burger, chips, cake, etc. as I believe that if they are completely deprived of these foods, they may go mad and gorge on them when they are later fending for themselves. Instead I taught them about good, balanced nutrition, with the occasional treat. Likewise, during the normal course of the week, they rarely had fizzy drinks and sweets, but had a small amount of sweets at the weekend and the occasional fizzy drink if we went out or had a special event. Some dieticians refer to this as the 90 per cent rule, in that 90 per cent of your diet is healthy. I truly believe that sugar, the wrong types of fats, salt, food colourings and additives are not only bad for the body, but can induce hyperactivity which can lead to bad behaviour. Likewise I know that white bread clogs and slows down the digestive system and is probably the worst thing you can give a child for lunch, as the main focus of the body will be on digesting bread, which instantly turns back to dough when combined with digestive juices. What you really want your child to do is to concentrate on her school work for the rest of the day.

As already mentioned, the boys are under weight for their age and are incredibly active, whereas Chris and I constantly face the 'battle of the bulge'. So we were able to use this as a way of educating the boys about how they would turn out later in life and the challenges they would face (in that it is a real drag to be constantly watching your weight) if they strayed too far from the regime I implemented for them. I also introduced a supplement of omega 3 fish oil into their diet and started to take this myself in order to gauge its effectiveness. As I had immediate results, in that I felt more alert, and over time their attention and results improved at school, I have continued with this to date.

Chapter 3

Some of the Realities of Settling In

Within days of them moving in we were beginning to see the full range of the boys' often bizarre behaviours. They challenged us constantly, frequently testing the boundaries. They were disrespectful of us and our property. We started asking them if this was the way they behaved on the farm, which always provoked an immediate and indignant, 'No' (as if they would even dream of behaving like that there!). This kind of made sense as we later learned that while they were in foster care they told us that they did attempt to behave as they knew that their foster homes weren't to be permanent and they feared being moved on. It soon became apparent to us that whatever the boys had learned whilst in their foster homes was now completely forgotten as they moved in with us.

From this we were able to deduce that almost right from the start they were relating to our house as home and were reproducing the kind of behaviours that they displayed back in their birth home, where their behaviour always went unchecked and usually unnoticed, and of course they had never been taught properly in the first place. To them, this is what 'home' meant and they couldn't understand why their behaviour was not acceptable. In a way I suppose it was a twisted kind of compliment, in that they were assuming that if it had been all right for them to behave like they had in their birth home, it must be all right for them to behave like that with us. We also chose to make it mean that it was a good sign that they were feeling comfortable and beginning to accept us, even if it wasn't in the way that we would have liked.

At other times they seemed to be getting at us and playing games. They were expert in finding our weak spots and picked at them savagely. Everything was a contest either between themselves, between them and us, or between us and Linda, or to some extent between Tony and their former lives. They lied convincingly about all the great stuff and times they had back then. Luke defended Linda brutally and couldn't bear that we might think badly of her. He was expert in creating situations where no matter what we did we would always turn out to be the losers and in the wrong. He constantly tried to trip us up and was keen to point out if we had made a mistake. He had very low self-esteem, thought he was ugly, and had no sense of humour. If anyone laughed in the same room as him he would become paranoid that everyone was laughing at him and have a tantrum. He totally dominated Adam and used him as his punch bag.

Adam thrived on this, as it made him into the victim and supposedly the 'good boy' in our eyes, earning more attention from us. (It was much later of course that we understood all of this and realized that half the time he was egging Luke on to make this happen.) Adam constantly looked to Luke to parent him. Although he danced and skipped around the house, we realized that he was living in a 'fantasyland'; in the real world he had no voice and no real personality. I would often lose him, only to find him standing right behind me in my 'blind spot' since he was so tiny. It was as if he chose to stand there, hidden from view, because this was his normally accepted place to be. This is what was comfortable for him.

Luke wanted to control him, us and every situation and frequently told us what to do. We found it amazing that for someone who found it so important to be controlling, his behaviour was often wild and out of control. We were also very worried about the inappropriateness of his approaches to strangers and the amount of trust he put in them and his almost adult interactions with family, friends and neighbours. The longer the boys stayed with us the more we realized that they didn't need the type of parents we had initially expected them to need. They needed us to be tough with them, to create firm boundaries and they desperately needed us to fight their corner. We gave ourselves a reality check and rapidly looked to ourselves and rethought our way of parenting them.

We realized almost immediately that Luke was going to need therapy. His behaviour was weird and changed constantly. What he knew one moment he seemed to have forgotten the next. There was no consistency in his day, his school work, his actions or abilities and no balance in his life. At times he was extremely clumsy; at others he was violent – often towards Adam, sometimes towards us, sometimes towards the other children at school and frequently hit himself (really hard) on the forehead, when he was displeased with himself. Out of all of his dire behaviours it was his inability to remember things from one moment to the next that bothered us most. It was almost as if he had several completely different personalities...still we always did intend to have a large family! We felt almost as though he needed to be broken down and then built up again.

We recognized that we would not only have to develop what we came to call 'fire fighting' techniques, but that we would have to deal with the underlying issues for both boys too. Of course the effect of all this behaviour started to take its toll on us. We began to doubt our ability to cope and despaired of ever getting it right. There were many dashes to the bathroom in the early days with me sobbing that 'I can't do this any more'. Although Chris didn't escape the effects of the boys' behaviour, most of it seemed to be directed at me. I felt awful. I was beginning to dread getting up in the mornings and dreaded picking them up from school even more. Occasionally for the sake of my own sanity, I had to put them to bed at six o'clock.

Yet even during the very darkest moments, we never hit or smacked them, even though we were sometimes tempted and came pretty close to it once or twice. We both knew that we were totally committed to straightening these boys out. We were determined that we were not going to cause them any more problems to add to their already very heavy sacks of baggage; we were always going to be there for them and we were going to stand up for them. I will give reasons, and suggestions, for coping with challenging behaviour later in the book.

Behaviour charts

Out of sheer desperation, I created a behaviour chart for each of the boys. I split this up into time periods, giving an alternative option for weekends:

- from getting up to arriving at school/from getting up till end of breakfast
- arriving at school to start of break/after breakfast to elevenses
- break/elevenses
- end of break till lunchtime/end of elevenses to lunchtime
- lunchtime
- after lunch till break/till afternoon tea break
- after break till home time/afternoon tea break
- arriving home till dinner time/after tea break till dinner time
- dinner time
- dinner time till bed time.

I kept this chart simple by awarding a star for each period of the day that they handled well, with a possible ten stars to be attained each day. Allowing them to put their own stars on the chart kept them interested and involved in the process, which in turn helped them to want to improve.

Progress charts for school

Unfortunately Luke's behaviour at school was erratic and disruptive to the rest of the class. Favourite traits were: getting up out of his chair, rocking on his chair, fiddling with things, talking, and singing out loud at totally inappropriate times. We later learned that all of these things were done to hide the fact that he didn't understand the lesson being taught and that he didn't like being put on the spot. This was his strategy for surviving in the classroom.

To give him consistency between his home and school life, each year I talked to his teacher and explained the need for continuity in the form of a progress chart. Each of his teachers made the chart differently – I really left it up to them. One year he was given ticks and stickers for different targets, devised to monitor particular aspects of his behaviour, and a treat to work for at the end of the week. One teacher targeted him for staying in his chair and putting up his hand to answer questions, instead of blurting them out every time a question was asked, preventing other children from having a go. She also provided a 'special table' close to her where he could ask to sit whenever he felt unsafe or felt the need to be alone. Another teacher provided a chart where he was monitored on his performance for each lesson with a smiley/sad/straight-mouthed face, with a space for comments. The best teacher he had not only provided a chart but told me daily how he had done. She was so patient, effective and interested in him that she even attended an Adoption Day event with us, where the children got to do activities while the adults attended a talk about adoption and education.

Having a progress chart at school had the additional benefit of my finding out exactly how his day had gone, which meant that I was able to incorporate the results attained at school onto his home progress chart, give suitable rewards/consequences and address any of the serious issues as they occurred. It also helped us to identify his most common behaviours, set targets for Luke to work towards and find ways of resolving some of his issues which helped him, his teacher and the rest of the class.

Reward 'nice' behaviour

At the same time as giving consequences for the boys' bad behaviour (see Chapter 10) it was also necessary to recognize and have them recognize their 'nice' behaviour. We started noticing all the things that they did well and told them in an enthusiastic voice when we thought they had done something nicely (though please note my comments on self-sabotage).

Children respond well to reward charts and there are all sorts of ways of using these. Be inventive. Use them in a way that is relevant to the child. I have seen many different methods and some fantastic ideas on parenting programmes on television and heard about many more from the people I've met on the courses I have attended. You could try awarding buttons or counters, putting them in a jar for each thing well done throughout the day. Then remind the child at bedtime what each button or counter was awarded for. Some people give the child 20 pennies at the beginning of the day and then take them away each time the child is naughty to see how many they end up with at the end of the day. With this method I would prefer to be giving the pennies back for even the slightest sign of nice behaviour, otherwise it is only focusing on the bad stuff. In fact, in my mind it would be better if the child were starting the day with no pennies and building upwards from there, focusing on nice behaviour only.

I know all too well how hard this stage of their development is, and if you are at this stage at the moment you have my support. I know that it is just as hard for you as it is for them. I am trying to give you a framework to work from. Please stick with it. Be strong. It has worked with my boys. The benefits are huge – just be aware that there is no quick fix, but persistence certainly does pay off.

Praise/self-sabotage

Accepting praise has always been hard for Luke. I suspect that this was something to do with his belief that he was intrinsically a 'bad child' – so much so, that he often ripped up his work or managed to spill something on it when over-praised at school, much to the horror of his teachers. Likewise we started to notice that if he had a particularly good day, either at school or at home, this would often be followed by a bout of bad behaviour shortly afterwards. To avoid him self-sabotaging, I found it better not to praise him directly, but to put the emphasis on the task he had just completed, with comments like, 'Great job with the dishes Luke', and 'The garden is looking nice – I like the bit that you did'. I also created what I can only call a 'strange' language, for the times when he brought a painting or piece of work home from school:

LUKE: What do you think of this, Mum?

ME: Well what do you think of it?

LUKE: I think I did a great job and I am really proud.

ME: Well, if you are proud then I am really pleased that you are proud.

LUKE: And I am really pleased that you are pleased that I am proud, [he'd answer jokingly].

I also found that it was better not to be too enthusiastic about a piece of work, so if asked for my opinion I would be direct: 'Well, I like this bit here (or the colour) and I think you have gone slightly wrong with this bit', or, 'I don't think that this is your best painting dear, I've seen you do much better before'. To avoid putting him down when he thinks he's done well I often answer by asking him how he thinks he's done. I know it sounds harsh, but he responds far better to honesty than gushing praise. I also think that he must know when he hasn't done his best, so for me, lying would not be the best policy as at this stage it is all about building trust. The thing about praise is to remember you are not necessarily dealing with someone who has learned to process praise normally. Having stuck with this, I now find that for the most part he can accept as much praise as I can give and he tells me that he loves pleasing me, getting my approval and the 'proud feelings' he gets now. It always made me feel very sad that he couldn't accept praise and receive encouragement as others can, but by sticking with it and over time he eventually got over his need to self-sabotage.

Schedule of daily routine

Had we known back then everything we know now we would have done several things differently. One of the things we bitterly regretted was not having introduced the boys to a daily schedule of routine much earlier, which we made big and bold and stuck to one of the kitchen cupboard doors for all to read. In fact we could have introduced this from day one. When we did eventually introduce it, we saw the boys respond almost instantly in a very positive way. It served to help them feel safe, know what to expect (taking the fear out of the unknown), work within a frame of reference, gave them uniformity and order, and stopped them trying to jump straight to the fun stuff, like watching television. It helped massively with their organizational skills and mine too. Rarely was anything forgotten and homework got done because the schedule said that this was what they needed to do. They could see in advance that they were always going to be fed and cared for and there was going to be time for fun each day.

For weekends and holidays, just having the bare bones of a schedule on the wall, or a more detailed schedule for special events like Christmas and birthdays, served to show them that whatever we chose to do, they were still going to be fed and looked after. This took away most of their anxiety and helped them to manage change and build trust between us. A word of advice, though, when making a schedule – remember that it is there to serve you and enable you to fit in everything you need to do. It is not open to discussion with the children. You are the parents, not them.

Creating a structured routine is of even more importance if you are holding down a job, are a single parent, have other children or have even more things you need to add to the equation. If this is the case, then the need for you to be organized and for your child to see that they will be properly cared for is perhaps even more critical.

Of course, by now our kitchen was beginning to look like the walls in their school. If people we knew came round who knew that they were being adopted, the boys didn't seem to mind, but I could see them becoming very anxious when the plumber came to look at a leak under the sink. So when he asked what all the notices were for I told a white lie to protect their dignity. I said that I was doing some work with 'other' children and that I was trying out some ideas on my own children first. He obviously believed what I said as he then asked me for some advice on his own child. I don't normally advocate the telling of any lies, but in this instance I'm glad I did, as the children really appreciated it. Shortly after this I had the same thing happen when three of their friends came to play. When I told them the same white lie, they were so interested and thought the various charts looked such fun that they actually sat down and talked about their own behaviour and what did and didn't work for them!

Introducing rituals, creating consistency

We introduced funny little rituals into our day-to-day life, like we always said the same thing each night as we put them to bed, 'Goodnight, sweet dreams', and as we were walking downstairs called out, 'I love you both'. Every night as we gave them a bath, we made beards and gave them silly hairdos out of the bubbles, which they thought was hilarious. Each time I finished combing their hair, I would look them in the eye declaring, 'You are absolutely gorgeous', whilst simultaneously tapping their nose with my forefinger. I would then give them a kiss on the lips. It's the silly little things like this that make a difference and helped them to feel that they belonged. I also made sure I planted the seed really early that we were all going to end up loving each other. I did this by stating, within a few days of their moving in, that I could see that I was going to find it really easy to love them, as I tucked them into bed and said goodnight. I was then able to progress and say that I thought I was beginning to love them, which of course was quickly followed by the real thing.

We created rituals and family traditions for Christmas, Easter and birthdays too. For example, on the first birthday, which happened to be Adam's, I hid all his presents around the house and he had to go looking for them. In a similar vein, on Luke's birthday I changed it into a treasure hunt with clues hidden around the house, which eventually brought him back to the lounge and his presents. On Adam's next birthday, we blindfolded him and took him to the lounge, where there was just one balloon. On taking the blindfold off he nearly burst out crying until he realized that inside the balloon was his first clue. At Christmas we always open stockings together in our bed, before going downstairs for the *real* presents and at lunch I always lay the dining table with our best crockery and crystal wine glasses and let them use them too. They were literally 'gobsmacked' the first time we let them do this and they did extremely well and declared that, 'We've never been allowed to use the "best" glasses before'. They often talk fondly of the things we get up to in 'our family'. Luke commented only the other day that he was definitely in the right family as we are as mad as him, the whole family is bonkers, and that he didn't know that living in this family would be such fun.

On a practical note, I always made sure I had a long list of possible things to do during the school holidays, so that no matter what the weather, how the boys were behaving or how I was feeling, we always had something to do. The first summer they were with us, we purposely didn't have a holiday, but chose to have 'days out' instead. I thought it would be nice if they had a record of all the things we got up to, so together we made a diary of everything we did in a large scrap book. I did most of the writing, but they added pictures and bits of relevant information, like entrance tickets, photos and postcards. I planted some sunflower seeds in the garden, told them they were magic beans, and then once a week they measured their growth and recorded it in their diaries. They were thrilled with the outcome and were very proud to show their scrap books to everyone they could.

To address the more serious issue of their past and the effect that it had had on them, I told them soon after they moved in that I/we would spend time with them and help them understand everything that had happened to them, as we felt that it wasn't good to avoid talking about their former lives. I told them that once they had come to terms with what had happened to them, they would start to feel better and could then go on and enjoy the rest of their lives, that we would make it as easy as possible for them, and that the thought of doing this needn't be another thing to worry about, as we would always make sure that they felt good about themselves after each session. We quickly confirmed this by introducing them to some of the exercises featured in this book, thus showing them that there really was nothing to fear. Consequently this became known as 'mum work' or 'dad work' and became something that they were happy to do as they liked to make sense of their pasts, felt that they were growing as people and enjoyed the huge sense of release through understanding that ensued. I will explain the exercises in more detail later in the book.

Mum time

It has been mentioned to me several times that children benefit from 15 minutes of 'special' time each day, when the child gets to play whatever she wants with her mother. This is a great suggestion as it not only helps bonding, but the child gets to see that no matter what she has done that day, she will always have that fun time. This, however, I found extremely hard to implement at first as having taken both boys at the same time they constantly vied for my attention and tried to sabotage any attention I might want to give to the other. I also found it extremely difficult, when they had just been horrible to me, to then play happily as if nothing had happened. It was quite some time before I was finally able to spend time with just one of them, so I had to find other ways of giving them those feelings. So 'mum time' in our house tended to mean doing painting, craft work, gardening, going for walks or playing board games. The important thing to remember is to build in 'fun' to the daily routine, as this will show that despite their bad behaviour, their lives are not just about receiving consequences and being told off.

To start off I set up a time after dinner to play with both children and built up to giving them individual time later on, when they were able to grasp that, just because I was spending time with one of them, didn't mean that I didn't love or wasn't interested in the other. When I was then able to spend time with each child individually, they learned that there was room in my heart for both of them. Since moving to our current house, we have discovered that our neighbour, who is a retired actress and is a very interesting and 'worldly' person (having raised a family of her own), likes to spend time with our children. Subsequently I was delighted when she asked if it would be all right to invite the boys to tea. They now take it in turns to go round each Sunday. They play all sorts of things together and she has put the emphasis on this being 'their' time. This in turn gives us the space to concentrate and give quality time to the other one.

Family night

One winner has proved to be 'family night'. This is quite simply Saturday night, but by naming it and referring to it as 'family night' it has taken on a special meaning for the boys. Through the week we always sit at the kitchen table to eat and are quite formal (in an attempt to develop their table manners and establish good eating habits), though more often than not Chris is not present at meal times due to the time he gets home from work. On Saturdays we always have a take away (to give me a break from cooking) and relax by eating and sitting in the lounge. The boys have little tables and Chris and I use trays. Afterwards we have sweets, which are considered a treat, as I don't usually allow them any during the week. Our children have an amazing, possibly unique, attitude to sweets which I can honestly say I have never met in another child. I usually give them a selection of sweets in a bowl, and it never ceases to amaze me that, after a while, they say, 'Who wants my sweets? I've had enough now!' We always watch Saturday night television, or if there is nothing worth watching, a video or DVD. Invariably we all end up cuddled together on the settee, which is great for bonding. It is wonderful to see how much family night now means to them as they have gone as far as turning down invitations to parties (though we don't encourage this) so they don't miss that favourite night of the week when they can relax with their family.

Chapter 4

Early Steps, Chores and Tasks

Almost from the beginning I set the boys jobs to do. (Jobs can easily be included in the daily schedule.) These days, they automatically ask if there is anything I want them to do when they have finished their homework, or at any time they see me struggling to do too many things at the same time. In fact, sometimes they don't even ask; I just find them helping out. Part of this stems from my desire to raise the kind of men who iron their own shirts and help around the house, but mainly it stems from my desire to let them know that I consider it to be their duty and that this is what being part of a normal family is. They need to know that I am not going to be their 'dog's body' and, if nothing else, they will know how to look after themselves in years to come.

The tasks I set were, and still are, age-appropriate and simple, for example: laying the table (explaining that the neater they did it, the more inviting it looked and how it was an essential part of presenting food nicely); taking stuff upstairs for me; emptying the dishwasher; dusting and polishing; making their own beds (a continuance of what they'd done in their last foster home); and helping with lots of chores in the garden (and again, from their foster home, reiterating the simple rule, 'If you make a mess you clear it up'). I encouraged them to take pride in their work by involving them with the day-to-day chores.

These days they have progressed massively and I am now teaching them to cook and help with the washing, ironing and hoovering. As we now live very close to the high street, and they are older, they regularly go to the shops for small items for me. Having said all this, please don't think that I am over-hard on them. Most of the chores I give them take just a few minutes and, if they have lots of homework or are going out, then I don't ask for any help at all.

Over time they began to take better care of our property and garden and enjoyed the sense of satisfaction that comes when you have done a good job. Luke was thrilled when I recently let him paint the garden shed. By allowing them to plant their own seeds and plants, water them and watch them grow, they became a bit less reckless when playing outside. After all, they had put the work in, so why wreck it? This also served to give them a sense of belonging, that this was *their* home. By doing work together and having something to focus their attention on (especially when gardening) it freed them up to talk honestly and openly about their experiences and former lives, which in turn made them keen to help in the garden more often, as it served as a form of therapy and release for them. A word of warning, though, please don't be tempted to offer your children money for the jobs they do, especially in the early stages, as this dilutes the valuable lessons that can be learned, unless of course they need to earn money as part of a consequence.

Team work

Doing chores together allowed us to discuss the benefits of working together as a team, not just in the garden, but in life in general. They now recognize that, if we all work together on the same side, we can achieve a lot more in life and that we all benefit from the results. Talking this through with the children I was able to point out that being in a family is very much like being on a team in that we all have slightly different roles/positions to play. So in our family Chris is the bread winner: he goes out and earns the money so that the rest of us can live a decent life, pay the bills, eat, buy things, etc. My role as mum is to manage the house, look after the children and generally make sure that everything runs smoothly and that everyone has what they need to do whatever they are doing. Then Luke and Adam's roles are to concentrate and do well at school and help mum and dad out when they need it.

The better we perform our individual roles, and the more aware we are of what each other is doing and their needs, the better we function as a team and the better we function as a family. I then pointed out that if one of the team players is weak, because they are ill for example, to keep the team strong the rest of the team needs to rally round and help that player/team mate and give him/her lots of support. I also pointed out that in this team there is plenty of room for individual success in that when one of us does well then we can all celebrate, as it is not only an achievement for that person, but is also an achievement for the whole team. Although sometimes it is great to score a goal, sometimes the team is more effective if we are not afraid to keep passing the ball to each other.

The loving step

One day, not long after the boys moved in, I went to pick them up from school as usual. Luke was looking particularly downcast and shame-faced. I knew instantly that something was wrong, but waited till we got home before dealing with it. Asking him what the matter was, he of course refused to answer. I knew I had to do something as he was obviously in agony. So I took him to sit on the third stair. I told him that from now on, this step was going to be called the 'loving step' and that on this step it was all right for him to tell me anything he wanted and that no matter how bad his action was, I wouldn't give him any consequences. Realizing that he was still unable to speak, I encouraged him further. I told him that I suspected that he thought he had done something very wrong and that he must think it was terribly bad, as he was finding it so hard to tell me. I then assured him that no matter how bad it was, or how bad he thought it was, I loved him and understood how difficult it was for him to tell me. I then promised him that even though he might not think it was the case, he would feel better when he had told me what he'd done.

I then reminded him of the time he'd dislocated his thumb and how I had taken him to hospital and how painful that had been. I reminded him that the pain had been so bad that he let the doctor pull his thumb about and put it back into place for him and that, even though it had been excruciating, from the moment he had done it, the pain started to subside and he felt better.

He was then able to tell me that he'd done a silly thing at school. He'd scratched his name onto a brand new chair with a screw. To his amazement, I immediately praised him for having the guts to tell me the truth, because I knew how hard that was for him. I told him that, just as I'd promised, I was not going to give him a consequence. However, if the school decided to give him one, then he would have to grit his teeth and take it like a man. He flung his arms round me, burst into tears and told me I was the best mum in the world and that he loved me, and I cried and hugged him too. From then on, he often asked if we could sit on the loving step, as he was in trouble at school a lot back then, but I always kept my promise, no matter what he'd done. These days he nearly always tells me the truth, and if he does forget and tries to lie, I just have to give him a look and he opens up and tells me the truth.

Early sex lessons

One day I could hear a lot of out-of-control giggling from upstairs. I knew immediately that the boys were up to no good. Racing up the stairs I found them literally emulating sex, with Luke 'riding' Adam in the 'doggy' position. Keeping a clear head I asked them what they were doing. 'We're pretending to have sex of course!' Luke answered raucously, which of course was exactly the answer I was dreading. To put this in perspective, they were seven and five at the time and had been with us for only a couple of weeks. Somehow I managed to stay calm. I told them to go and sit at the patio table whilst I made drinks to give me a moment to think and collect myself. Going out to join them I asked where they had learned about sex. They told me that they had watched Linda have sex on a number of occasions. I asked if they had ever been involved, which they thought was hilarious (thankfully). I then told them that she really shouldn't have let them see. Luke of course immediately leapt to her defence, saying that they just used to walk in without thinking.

I then explained that sex was a thing that adults do, but it's not all right to do it at their age as their bodies weren't ready. I told them that if they wanted to touch themselves they must do that alone in their own rooms and that it was not all right to touch each other or anyone else. I then talked to them about the inappropriateness of touching children at school, for example, and that they would get into a lot of trouble if they tried it. I also advised them that it wasn't right to talk about sex to other children, as most children didn't know about sex at their age and their parents wouldn't like it if they told them everything they knew. I still wonder to this day at how I managed to stay so calm and collected as I couldn't believe that after having the boys live with me for just two weeks I was sitting in my garden giving sex lessons to a five and seven-year-old.

In a similar vein, and about the same time, I had to deal with Luke's inappropriate kisses. I felt almost as if he was making advances towards me, which made my flesh creep. For a little while I had to stop him kissing me until he learned more about mother/son relationships and I felt unable to kiss him as it still made my flesh crawl. Knowing how important it was that we got past this, I found I was able to kiss him on the top of his head and then on his cheek again, building up to hugs and a quick kiss on the lips. (That's what we do in our family.) Then if he started being inappropriate again, I would tell him that that is not the type of kiss that you give a mum, please don't do that again. Thankfully he quickly got over this.

Over-competitiveness

We noticed straight away just how competitive the boys were, not just with themselves whilst playing, but with absolutely everyone and everything. They were so competitive that a simple game of something like snakes and ladders would end up with us feeling as though World War Three had started. So I started changing the rules of some games so that they learned to enjoy playing together just for the sake of having fun. For example, with snakes and ladders, we sometimes begun at the end and ended at the beginning, or went up the snakes and down the ladders. With ludo, two of us went the normal way round the board and two of us went the other way. I would sometimes give each of us a number then write the numbers on a piece of paper and fold them up. Then I'd pick a number and produce it at the end of the game. This person was then declared the winner, regardless of where they had finished in the game. Sometimes I would announce the first winner, then the second winner, followed by the third and fourth winners, followed by the statement that there are no losers in this house! With everything else we constantly told them that, 'It's not a race.' 'It's not a competition.'

Choice

I'm afraid to say I learned about 'choice' the hard way. One day, as a treat, I took Luke to the supermarket to choose a pudding. The poor boy was totally confused as we found there were two aisles of frozen puddings and ice creams, two rows of dry and packaged cakes and puddings, the baker counter and a chiller cabinet full of cream cakes and puddings. He ran up and down each aisle literally pulling his hair out. What was supposed to be a treat was definitely not having the effect that I intended. In the end I picked up two items that I knew he liked and asked him which he would prefer. After that, I started limiting his choices.

I later learned that choice is a definite issue for traumatized children. Luke would often not want to take responsibility for his choices and would try and pass the onus back to me saying, 'I don't know what to choose, Mum, you choose for me'. I saw this as an opportunity for him to learn something. I told him that I appreciated that making choices was hard for him, yet I wanted him to start taking responsibility for his choices. I pointed out that if I made the choice for him, he could get to blame me if it turned out to be the wrong choice and that that wasn't fair. So in future he needed to make his own choices, otherwise he would never learn. He needed to learn to make his own choices, even if he got it wrong sometimes, as in order to learn he needed to experience what making the wrong choice felt like. I pointed out that life is full of choices and opportunities and one day when he needed to make a choice I might not be there to advise him, which is why he needed to learn about them for himself. I told him that a good way to start would be for him to consider what the outcome or consequence would be for each choice he was faced with (the lesson here is obviously a lot deeper than just picking the right pudding) and then make his decision according to what he felt was best.

I then pointed out that Dad and I would always be available to discuss any of the really big decisions he needed to make in life, but for now the object of the exercise was to get him used to the process of making a decision for himself, and the way to do this was to start with the small, unimportant things, like choosing a pudding. We found we needed to limit the boys' choices, especially Luke's, for quite a long time. We were then able gradually to increase them. However, every now and again Luke slips back into his old way of being and I have to remind him gently that he is being lazy by putting the responsibility for his choices onto someone else.

Peripheral vision

Not long after the boys moved in we realized that Luke lived in a permanent state of hypervigilance. This was because, in order for him to feel safe, he needed to know everything that was happening – hence his need to eavesdrop on our conversations. He was often in trouble at school because he was nearly always 'at the scene' when naughtiness occurred. It took us quite some time to realize that this was because he needed to be there, to see what was going on, so that he could feel safe. He often tried to intervene when trouble broke out, as he could see when other children were doing the wrong thing and would try to stop them, but of course, because he was then involved himself, he subsequently got into trouble when an adult got involved.

An example of this was when he was hauled in front of the head because he threw a rock over the school fence, narrowly missing a passer-by. It was only when I sat down to talk about it later on the 'loving step' that I found out that some other children had been throwing rocks at each other and that Luke had got involved because he knew that this was wrong. He had confiscated a rock for safety purposes and had forgotten to be more careful in the way that he had disposed of it. With this in mind we started to recognize just how anxious and stressed Luke was, and that every time he went anywhere he needed to survey the scene to see if there was any trouble and investigate it if there was. He needed to look for a sensible adult and make himself known, so that he would know who to go to if he needed protection, and he needed to look for exits if he went into a new building in case he needed to get out in a hurry.

Understanding all this I was then able to teach the boys about peripheral vision. I drew a diagram of how a lot of people used their vision and only looked at things straight on. I then told them that it was possible to see everything within a 180 degree radius and demonstrated this by asking them to put their arms straight out to the sides at shoulder height and then look at both their hands at the same time. If your child is one of those people who have only experienced 'tunnel vision', this really can be

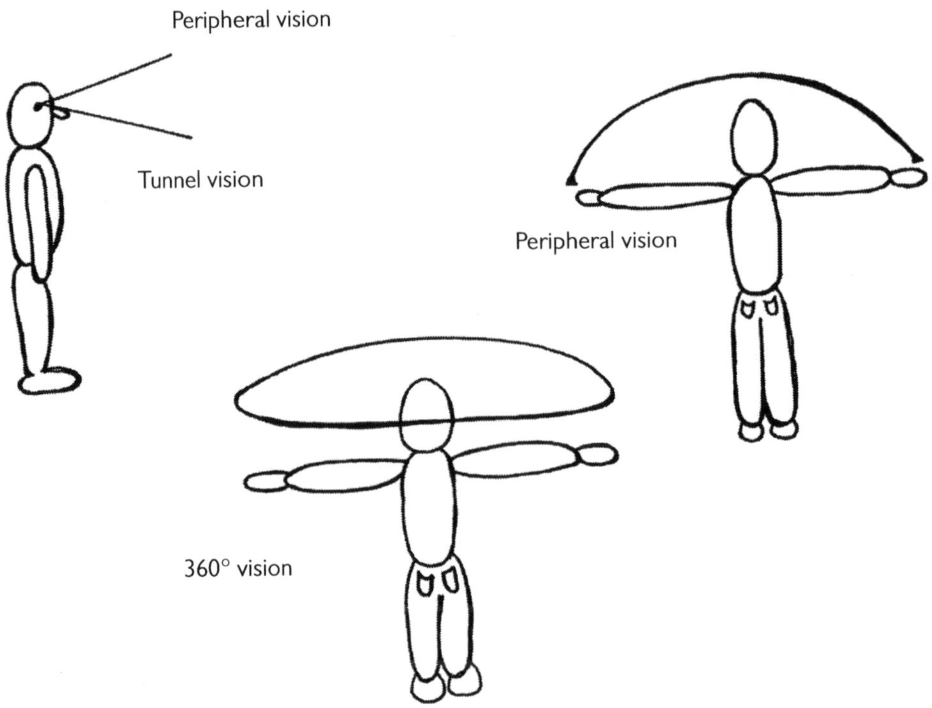

Figure 4.1: Peripheral vision

quite a revelation for them. I then asked them to hold their arms out at shoulder height again and this time to imagine that they could see right round in a full circle behind them. This exercise is great for beating hypervigilance. It has such a powerful calming effect that it will work if your child is walking into a room of strangers or if she is faced with exam nerves. Giving her this distinction is a real gift as she will be able to contain her nerves and she will be unable to go back to seeing in her old 'tunnelled vision' way. It is as if the world suddenly opens up for her and she can 'see' that it isn't such a scary place.

Making friends

Many children have trouble making and keeping friends. It seems even harder if you don't like yourself, feel that you are bad and unworthy of being liked, think that you are different and that you don't belong. So soon after the boys moved in we started conversations about what we could do to have people like us and want to be our friends, what kind of people we wanted as friends and how we thought we might need to behave if we wanted to keep friends or invite them round to play. During these conversations we gave them some tips on how to have people like them:

- Each time you look at someone, get into the habit of finding something you like about them, perhaps what they are wearing, their hair style, eyes or the way they talk. It will be really hard for them not to like you if they know that you like them.
- Try telling them that you think they are funny, clever, smart, etc.
- Offer them a sweet.
- Find someone who looks lonely and ask them if they would like to play with you.
- Look for similarities between you and make comments about being the same.
- Find common ground and shared interests.
- Show that you are really interested in the other person. A good way to do this is to ask lots of questions. Most people love the opportunity to talk about themselves and will be even more impressed if you remember what they have told you and will really start to like you if you ask them how they got on with…or enjoyed their weekend.
- You could have a go at building rapport by 'matching' and 'mirroring'. This one will need a bit of practice because if you aren't good at this and the other person notices what you are doing they may well get annoyed. So it is advisable to practise a lot with your family until it becomes second nature. This technique works on the principle that if you are the same as or have similar characteristics to someone else they will like you because they like people who are similar to themselves – because you remind them of themselves and they like themselves!

- ‘Matching’ is the process of copying another’s mannerisms, movements or posture. For example: if they pick up a glass with their right hand, take a sip and then put the glass down and play with the rim, you would do the same or similar soon afterwards. If they cup their face in their left hand then you would do the same and if they cross their legs, you would again do the same. Their subconscious will then start to notice that you are similar and therefore worth liking.
- Mirroring is exactly the same except you would use this if you were sitting opposite each other, so it would be like looking in the mirror in that if they made a gesture with their right hand, you would mirror this by making a similar gesture with your left hand.

Once the boys were familiar with all these principles we then started practising having a friend round to play after school. This was easy for us, having two children, but if you only have one child you could pretend to be the friend. I did this by saying to Luke that I wanted him to pretend that he had invited his friend Adam round to play after school and that he was to look after him, show him where everything was, make sure that he had a good time and to practise his new skills. Then I told Adam that he was to pretend that he was Luke’s friend and that he had never been to our house before. Next time we swapped their roles round and repeated the process. If you have more children you could practise how they would treat the friend too. It wasn’t long before we were able to invite real friends home.

Early lessons in time-keeping

At around the same time as this we also started getting them used to the idea that one day they would want to walk to school on their own, play with other children after school, go to the park on their own and eventually as teenagers go out in the evenings. To prepare the way for this I started by telling them they could play in the garden and that I wanted them to come and see me when the ‘big hand was on the three’. Needless to say they were very young and still couldn’t tell the time properly. At this stage it is all about getting them to start taking responsibility for their time-keeping and to do this they need to get used to looking at their watch. I repeated this exercise countless times. Each time they successfully reported in on time, I then allowed them to go out and play again and gave them a new check-in time. If they failed, I pointed out that if they had been playing at their friend's house or in the park, I would then be sitting at home worrying about them and that wouldn't be fair of them. I would then tell them that they had to come in, saying that maybe they would do better next time we practised this.

The next step was to let them play out with the other children who lived in our very quiet cul-de-sac. The rules were exactly the same, that they had to keep checking in with me, with the additional rule that if they wanted to go and play in one of the other children's houses, they must come and tell me first and agree a time to be home. They soon became very good at this and could clearly see how I would worry if they were late. Only recently have I allowed them to take this a stage further by occasionally letting them go to the park on their own. This has only been in broad daylight and on the condition that they ring me at regular intervals. Telling a friend how I had taught the boys to be responsible in this way, she said that she was amazed and had never heard of anyone going to such lengths. She quickly added that she was really impressed and wished that all parents took that effort with their children. I have to say that I agree with her and was quick to point out that I did this as it also helped the boys to feel safe and, if nothing else, at least they knew that they had someone who cared enough to worry about them.

In conjunction with this I started pointing out potential dangers on the walk to school, how traffic moved, where the best places to cross the road were and how it was safest to walk along the pavements with as much space as possible between them and the road and what to do if someone tried to give them a lift, offered them sweets, etc. The next step was for them to tell me all the commonsense things that they noticed on our walks to and from school. We extended this to trips up the high street to the shops, crossing busy supermarket car parks, going shopping in town and even did the same when we went into London. Having said that, it will be a very long time before I let them go there on their own! We did all this well in advance of it actually happening as we felt it was important that they became 'street wise' as soon as possible just in case of an emergency. The next thing I did was to have them take it in turns to cross us all over the road safely. I'm happy to report that we are still here to tell the tale. I then extended this to a complete trip to school and did the same in the High Street and the car park. I also had them learn our phone numbers, showed them where I kept our address books, explained to them what to do if Chris or I had an accident at home and they needed to get help, how to ring the emergency services and how to make a reverse charge call. This was all reiterated when they visited a safety centre with the school.

Eventually Luke did ask if they could walk home from school on their own. I said no for quite a long time, pointing out that it wasn't because I didn't trust them; it was because I didn't trust other potentially dangerous people out there. I wasn't happy at that time to let them cross the extremely busy road they would have to cross on their own, as there were no pelican crossings there. After we had settled into our current house and they had got used to the much quieter roads on the school route I did start letting them walk part of the way home and eventually all of the way. I mentioned earlier that Chris and I didn't believe in spoiling the boys, but I did insist at this point that Luke had a simple 'pay as you go' phone. It wasn't long before he was to start secondary school and we did the same for Adam the following year. Luke used it to tell me that he and Adam had arrived at school each day and that they had met each other after school and were then on their way home. Although this might seem overprotective to some people, to me this ties in with what I was saying about teaching the boys how to be responsible, not just for now, while they are still quite young, but when they are well into their teens.

Chapter 5

The Grieving Process

I have read several different interpretations of the grieving process. Most of them refer to the different stages or steps that need to be worked through. The following is one example:

1. shock
2. guilt
3. denial
4. depression
5. fear
6. anger
7. acceptance.

The important thing to remember is that each of us handles grief differently. We may well follow the various stages as suggested, but not necessarily in the same order or intensity as the next person. There is quite simply no right or wrong way to do it. It is also important to know that children who are taken into care may find it difficult to express their emotions and can only do so through their behaviours, which can be quite bizarre (see Chapter 8).

It may well be that your child has suffered the loss of one or both parents, and needs to be allowed to work through the various stages of grief. However, a lot of children placed in care are there for quite different reasons but, just as with loss through death, they may well need to go through a similar process as they have 'lost' their former lives and their identities have consequently been badly shaken. This is known as adaptive grieving. They need time to grieve the loss of their former lives while they adapt to their new surroundings and way of life.

The most important thing is to acknowledge that your child is feeling sad. Giving her your permission and reassurance that it is all right to feel this way will go a long way towards her healing, her bonding and her building trust in you. Children who don't deal with their sense of loss may eventually get very good at 'pretending' that everything is all right. By denying them the right to this process it will force them to keep a 'secret' about their unresolved grief and separation from their birth family, and this can lead to all sorts of problems and resentments in later life. With this in mind, we have no secrets in our house, except when keeping birthday or Christmas presents a surprise.

There are several things that can ease the child's pain during this period, and most of these will benefit any child dealing with either loss of parent(s) or loss of former lives:

- allowing the child to have photos in their room
- making life story books
- treasure boxes for their keepsakes
- putting a message in a balloon and sending it to heaven
- visiting the deceased's grave
- saying prayers for either deceased parents or birth parents
- scattering flowers or petals on water
- lighting candles
- writing poetry or letters
- drawing pictures or painting
- recreating stories with soft toys about what happened
- making a cartoon-type story about what happened
- talking freely about what happened
- contact with birth parents
- letter contact with birth parents
- just being there for the child

- writing letters on the computer, and actually making up your own replies, or better still have the child make up what they think the reply might be
- helping the child to create a 'special room' in their minds for remembering, which they can open and close the door to as often as they like
- and of course bucket loads of patience, understanding, empathy and listening on your part.

We felt a bit uncomfortable about having photos of Linda and Tony on display, but recognized that this was necessary for the grieving process, and it wasn't long before the photos found their way to the bottom of the toy box.

Much as Chris and I would have liked to wrap the boys up in cotton wool to protect them from life, unfortunately – as we all know – this is not possible. So when one of their close school friends died after being hit by a car, we were extremely anxious about how they would cope. This was obviously not a pleasant experience for them, especially as they were held up in traffic on the way back from a karate lesson as the air ambulance flew in. Thankfully they handled it far better than we expected with Adam sobbing his heart out soon after we heard the news and Luke following suit a day later. We handled this by allowing them to talk about it as much as they wanted to, and each time one of them needed a hug or said that they missed him we said that we understood, that it was natural to feel like that.

When Adam, who was probably closer to him than Luke, still seemed sad after a few weeks I asked him if he thought his friend would want him to keep on feeling unhappy, and then suggested that he might be more concerned about how the boy's surviving twin brother was coping and that he had a good friend to lean on, and that – perhaps rather than feeling sad – he could focus on being there for him. I then helped him with this by discussing with him the feelings that that boy might be having, how he would miss his brother all his life and the difficulties he might face when he went back to school and had to mix with and perhaps answer questions asked by the other children. Taking this on board, both boys were really sweet to him and I'm sure their sensitivity and sincerity made a difference to him.

Coping with special occasions

After three very difficult Mothering Sundays, Luke's therapist suggested that we hold a remembrance service. This was to satisfy the part of Luke that still wanted to be with Linda. I did this by lighting a candle. I then asked the boys to spend a few minutes thinking of (nice things only) about Linda, and even though they seemed unaffected when they spoke of their birth dad Tony, we repeated the process for him for good measure too. I then told them to close their eyes and imagine them both happy and getting on with their lives and doing well. We said a prayer asking God to look after them and to deliver the boys' love to them on their behalf. It worked brilliantly. Subsequently I now repeat this process prior to each Mothering Sunday and all have gone without a hitch, giving me the satisfaction of enjoying them as I had imagined they would be when I was first considering adoption. Likewise, I spend a few moments with them thinking of Linda and Tony just before birthdays and Christmas so that on the actual day, we are focusing on and enjoying the event only.

The second Christmas the boys were with us I made the mistake of thinking that they might be able to handle it if we gave them their presents from their birth family (other relations sent presents too) along with all their other presents on Christmas morning. That was a big mistake as Luke definitely couldn't handle it and had a massive tantrum. It was clear that by doing this he had been forced to remember all the issues he faced, on a day which he had been looking forward to and which he expected to be full of fun and pleasant surprises. To show his disapproval he consequently decided to let me know in no uncertain terms just how cross he was that I had spoiled his day by spoiling Christmas Day for the rest of us. I never made that mistake again.

Another difficult aspect we had to deal with was birthdays. It wasn't quite so bad for the child actually having the birthday, but Luke in particular found Adam's birthdays hard to handle, to the extent that on Adam's first birthday with us, which was soon after they moved in, he did everything he could think of to sabotage the day and switch the focus of attention away from the 'birthday boy' and on to him. This ranged from hitting Adam and having tantrums to breaking Adam's toys before he barely had a chance to look at them. Clearly we had to do something. Later, discussing this with his therapist, she suggested that we include him more in the preparation for the event, as a lot of the problem was a result of the stress he incurred with not knowing how the day would pan out and also because of his hatred of not being in on secrets.

So for Adam's next birthday I put the following into practice. I didn't want to make a schedule for the day and put it on the wall, as that would spoil all the surprises we had lined up for Adam, so I told Luke what was going to happen instead. Then I let him help me organize some of the party games and prepare the food. I also got him to help me light the candles on the birthday cake. For the next few birthdays I included a few small presents for the other child in the treasure hunt, which you might think was giving in, but as I did this for both boys it did solve the problem. After a couple of years I was then able to stop giving this extra present and explain why I did so.

Contact

The whole issue of contact with birth parents seems to me to be a tricky one. It appears that it is better for the child if they continue to have contact with their birth parents throughout the adoption as this helps them to:

- maintain a balanced and realistic view as to what they were like
- understand where they came from
- make sense of their past
- make the comparison to see that what they have now is better than that in the past
- overcome issues of identity
- deal with any anxiety they may have over the welfare of their birth parents
- avoid the frequent need for adopted children to seek out their birth parents when they are older.

Having said all this, there are still obviously many reasons why it is definitely not in the child's best interest to have contact, for example in the case of a child having to confront a violent and/or sexual abuser. In those cases contact isn't even suggested. Contact, in our opinion, is only advisable with birth parents if they wholeheartedly support the adoption, accept that their child has moved on and have relinquished any power or hold on them. If they can do this and accept that this is what is best for the child, they may well be on the way in their own healing process, but to do this they also need to accept responsibility for what went wrong.

Our own experience of contact proved to be extremely painful and negative and seemed only to confuse the boys in terms of who their parents are now and where they, and indeed their loyalties, belonged. So I have decided to share only a little of this with you so you are aware of some of the things that can go wrong and are properly informed when you are considering your child's needs.

For our children, contact was to be at six-monthly intervals. Who set this, when it was agreed and why it was deemed to be in their best interests we don't know, unless it was set this way because they might return to Linda. What we do know is that after each contact, the boys, especially Luke, reacted badly. He returned from each contact with Linda in what I can only describe as a manic state. He was highly flushed, totally over-excited and completely out of control. This all manifested itself in extremely bad and wild behaviour. For Adam, contact seemed to remind him that Luke was Linda's favourite, as he barely got a look in and was virtually ignored. This reminded him of all the feelings he used to have, which made him forget everything he had learned with us and go back to his old way of being, i.e. being bossed and parented by Luke. This was then reinforced when he saw Luke go back to *his* old way of being, and he would become incredibly reliant on him and also out of control, to the extent that he expected to be allowed to stay up all night watching television and would refuse to go to bed. For Luke it served to remind him that, yes, he had a former life, and whilst he was with Linda he was able to do whatever he liked, whenever he liked and his behaviour went unchecked. A huge part of him craved the freedom of that former life, so after this and every subsequent contact his behaviour deteriorated massively, so much so that it felt as though he had only just recovered from one contact and it was time to prepare him for the next.

After the first contact I spent a terrible and terrifying evening with him when he had what I can only describe as a near nervous breakdown. I found him pacing round his bedroom in a dazed, deranged state, literally pulling his hair out. I sat on his bed trying to get his attention by gently calling his name for what seemed like an eternity, before he was able to recognize that I was in the room with him. I eventually managed to calm him and got him to sit next to me and tell me what was going through his mind. He said that he didn't know what to do because he had all these people over here and all these people over there and he didn't know who he was supposed to love because he loved us and didn't want to hurt us and what he found very difficult to say was that he still loved them.

I told him that he had two families now and that I was trying very hard to understand how difficult that must be for him. I told him that it was all right for him to love both families and that we wouldn't be upset if he did this; in fact we had expected it and I was sure that he had enough room in his heart to love everybody. If he was finding it difficult to think of me as his mum, when he already had a mum, he could think of me as his best friend who was prepared to listen to him and help him get through this and make sense of it all. If he really wanted to, he could call me by my first name until he felt better about things. I am pleased to say that he didn't choose this option.

Next he said he wished he had a time machine so that he could go back and see his old life and family. I told him that that was an idea, though that would mean that he would have to go back and then live his whole life again, that he would find that things were just the same, and that he would have to go through all the same stuff and be taken into care again, only this time he would know what life was like with us. He then suggested that perhaps he could go back and take me with him, so that we could both have a look and that I would know what to do about it, and then we could come back together. I said that this was a much better idea and that although we couldn't really go back to his former life, when he was feeling stronger I would look at that life with him and help him come to terms with everything that had happened to him.

I then told him that I wished his life hadn't been so hard – in fact I wished that we hadn't even had the opportunity to adopt him, not because I didn't want or love him, but because I was so sad that all these things had happened to him and I genuinely wished that they hadn't. I then added, just for luck, that in fact I wished that there was no such thing as children being taken into care or adoption because I would prefer it if no child had to suffer in this way. We then hugged and cried together.

Not long after this Luke admitted to me that he was worried that he had moved even further away from Linda and it seemed to be really unsettling him. So I stuck a piece of paper on his bedroom wall and drew him a map, showing where Linda was, where his foster home was and where he now was with us which formed a triangle. Seeing that he was actually roughly the same distance away and it was just a different direction and that the triangle had just changed shape alleviated that particular fear for him, and just to prove that I wasn't lying, I also showed him our positions on a road map.

Had all this been an end to his inner turmoil it wouldn't have been so bad. However, as each contact loomed, Chris and I began to despair as we knew that we ourselves were going to have to pick up the pieces and live with their destructive out-of-control behaviour. Some experts might say that we transposed our fear on to them. This may to some extent be true, though I have never been able to work out how to mask our emotions completely, as it was us who had to live with the consequences. It is hard to describe to anyone who hasn't been in this position themselves the deep feelings of despair we felt having worked so hard to get the boys on an even keel, only to see them deteriorate to their original way of being in the space of a few hours.

We tried doing lots of work with them in preparation for each visit and when that didn't work tried not telling them till the last minute. No matter what we did, the outcome was always the same. Possibly one of the reasons that things went so wrong was that Linda and the boys were assigned a new social worker just after the boys moved in with us. She insisted that as Linda had somehow missed out on a contact they see her straight away. With hindsight we could see that seeing her so quickly confused things in their minds and that it would have been much better for them if they had been allowed a lot more time to get their feet well and truly under 'our table'.

Presents or no presents

At each contact Linda arrived armed with bin liners full of presents and huge bags of sweets for them. This clearly did them no good at all.

Contact for them became about the anticipation of presents, so that when asked they said they loved having contact with her – after all, what child doesn't like being spoiled? Birthdays and Christmas were no better either. The first Christmas they were with us proved to be a real learning experience, what with our family and friends wanting to spoil them and welcome them into the family and their birth family feeling guilty for them being taken away. They had so many presents that they had to open them in three sittings. They received no less than 19 selection boxes of chocolates each! Many of the presents were duplicated and the whole thing was obscene. We ended up having to give a lot of things to charity and the children's hospital. We vowed never to have a Christmas like that again, and I didn't care how guilty their birth family felt, lavishing them with presents was not the answer. I did not intend to bring up two spoilt little boys.

We then agreed with Linda and Tony – although Tony wasn't so bad in the present/spoiling stakes – that, at the suggestion of a social worker, for birthdays and Christmas they would give the boys either a book or a gift voucher and that they could send them through the letter box system, or that they could send us the money and a label and we would buy a suitable book. From then on the boys received nothing. It was only when we said no to presents that the children started to admit that actually they didn't really want to see Linda and Tony. We made various agreements with Linda, only to have her ignore them all and do her own thing and so we struggled on.

Maybe we should have stuck to our guns and refused point blank to carry on with something that seemed so damaging, but the boys weren't officially adopted by then, so we didn't want to rock the boat. I also thought that the 'experts' might be right and that having contact might be better for them in the long run, though I didn't know how much longer we were going to be able to cope with it. It was only after having the boys for two years, and they were adopted and in therapy, that anyone else (Luke's therapist) recognized that contact wasn't working for the boys, mainly because Luke told his therapist about some of the comments Linda had made about 'when he went back to her', what she had promised he would get to do on his return and how he'd only got to put up with us until he was 18. Contact was then frozen until such time as the boys wanted to restart it.

With Tony, contact was a little easier as Luke had little recollection of what living with him was like and Adam had no memory of this at all. Also Tony seemed altogether more sensible and was far more supportive of the adoption. However, contact with him seemed odd to say the least. It felt as if we were all going off to meet a stranger, who then played with them for an hour or two in the park, but they made no attempt to talk to him and get to know him, or vice versa. Once contact was frozen with Linda, seeing him seemed to replace the feelings that contact with her gave them and take them back to their old life and repeated patterns of behaviour. In due course this contact was frozen as well.

We have always left the door open for them, though, and every few months we ask the children if they feel ready to see them again. Luke is adamant that he never wants to see either of them again, though Adam has always said that he would like to see them both some time in the future to say goodbye, although we are unable to see how that might work. I recently asked them if they still felt the same. Luke did still feel the same and said in no uncertain terms, 'No, I don't want to see them. I am happy with my life the way it is. They had their chance and they blew it!' Adam, on the other hand, seemed genuinely shocked by Luke's statement. He thought that like himself, Luke would want to see them to find out if they were all right, and he couldn't understand how Luke had reached his decision. I then realized that Adam was ready and needed to do some of the work featured in this book again. He then asked if this is how he is supposed to feel and I reassured him that there was no right or wrong way to feel and that if he wanted to see them that would be all right with us. I then pointed out his options:

- We could arrange to see them.
- He could ring them.
- We could ring them.
- He could write to them.
- We could write to them as a family.

He didn't really like any of these ideas. He decided that, on the one hand, he wanted to see them to find out how they were but, on the other, he didn't know what to say to them and admitted that he was scared that seeing them would prompt him to return to his old behaviours and he didn't want to do that. I then had to tell him that we didn't really want to ring them either because both Linda and Tony had had our phone number for quite some time and that we had told them that they could ring us every three or four months if they wanted, but the truth was that Tony had never rung and Linda had rung once and that was nearly three years ago. We all needed some time to think about it. Then, after a couple of days, we decided that we would write to them as a family, but warned Adam that we might not get a reply and, if that was the case, he would just have to accept that.

Personally I would actually prefer it if they both saw both their birth parents sometime before they are 18 so that we can supervise them and stop them from being sucked back in, which is a real fear for me. If they seek Linda out after they are 18, she may well suck them back in, as to all intents and purposes, she seemed quite 'together' and charming the last time we saw her.

Our experience of contact was not, as I've already said, a positive experience. Perhaps contact was arranged in this way as it had been deemed to be in Linda's best interest. Unfortunately it seemed that she was only able to consider things based on her wants and needs and was unable to comprehend the needs of the boys. For example, when it came to showering them with presents, she said it was because she wanted to see the look on their faces. When loading them full of sugary sweets perhaps it was because she wanted to spoil them and look like the 'good guy' in their eyes and then couldn't understand it when at one of the first contacts Luke, hyped up and full of sugar, went over to a two-year-old and kicked him in the head. This apparently was my fault, even though I wasn't present at the time, as this contact was being supervised by their social worker and nothing to do with the fact that, during contact, Linda herself was supposed to be in charge of supervising them and being responsible for their behaviour. She even went as far as ignoring my advice (at another contact) not to let Luke go on the roundabout as he wasn't feeling well and was amazed when he was violently sick and was then deeply put out when he clung to me for the rest of the meeting.

Considerations for contact

With all the above in mind I urge you to approach contact with extreme caution and take care with your decision. Consider the following carefully, not just for now, but think of the years ahead:

- Do you truly understand what will be required of you?
- Ask yourself what you want to achieve from contact.
- Ask yourself for whom you are doing this (who will benefit?) and what's the purpose of it?

Take time to consider all the possible outcomes. Really think about where you want to have your contact. Will what you want to achieve involve a happy three-hour picnic in the park, or would the child's needs be best met in a one-hour meeting in a room supplied by social services? When we first went into adoption and 'open adoption' was mentioned, I had an idealistic picture of us having contacts in our own home, so that the birth parents could see how the boys had settled into their new home and way of life. This view was completely altered when it was pointed out to me that the children need to feel 'safe' in their new home, and to have their birth parents in their new home would be a violation of this. Having learned the hard way, I was able to see that the reasons why contact is a good idea would have been better met with a one-hour supervised visit in a room supplied by social services than in the venues that we chose, which proved to detract from the purpose of these meetings and perhaps had too much 'fun' attached to them.

Imagine yourself in different scenarios and 'test out' how they will work out and how everyone will feel afterwards. Ask yourself the following questions:

- Does the social worker work on behalf of your child and their birth mother? If so, how can this possibly be working in the best interest of your child?
- Does your child's social worker know your child and her case well?
- How can he/she make contact decisions if he/she doesn't know your child personally? He/she may well be familiar with the case history, as in our case, without knowing the child.

- Does your child like her social worker?
- Do you need to create ground rules between the birth parents and yourselves? These rules need to include who will take responsibility for making the arrangements and how. They should also include the logistics, lengths, times, frequency, location, supervision, who will be present (will other members of the birth family be included?) and whether presents, sweets, food, etc. will be allowed.
- Consider how the birth parents may react to your suggestions. You may have to get tough if they let you down with their side of the bargain.
- What does your child say about this?
- What does your gut instinct say about this?
- Carefully monitor any reactions the child may have during or after a contact.
- Don't be bamboozled into anything that you don't feel comfortable with.
- Remember you are responsible for your child and you probably know them better than anyone else by now.
- Consider the whole safety angle. Will you accompany your child and be present during each meeting and do you want a third person there?

You may also want to consider a few 'what if' scenarios at this time so that if something happens in the future you will be prepared. For example, in our own case Linda and Tony were separated long before the boys were taken into care, but at one point we were told that they had got back together again. You may want to consider how you would handle a visit if either birth parent formed new relationships, and what would happen if they then had children. Would you want your child to have a relationship with any new children? You may want to think about what you'd do if either of the birth parents were seriously ill, or died, and what you'd do if one or both of you died. What would be best for your child? I have no doubt in my mind that for some adoptive families contact can be worked out (it may not necessarily be easy to do) and it will be beneficial for the children. Likewise I know that contact isn't right for every child.

If contact is definitely out of the question you may wish to consider 'letterbox contact'. I would suggest that you ask yourself similar questions to those above if considering this. Our experience of letterbox contact was not good, in that I found it painfully difficult to write a 'nice' letter about everyday life and the boys' achievements when all I wanted to do was scream at both parents, 'Look what you've done to your children, see how they are suffering and the problems you've caused them!' I did, however, meet our end of the bargain only to have it thrown back in my face when Linda called Chris and told him that it was a load of rubbish. Hey ho! Good luck.

Chapter 6

Brain Development

I have compiled this information on brain development from the numerous courses I have attended. This information is also widely available on many websites and in countless books. It is meant as a rough guide as no two children will develop at the same rate or in exactly the same way nor will they experience the same set of circumstances. I found all this information useful as I knew little about the stages of a child's development before we entered into adoption. Whilst considering these stages, I noted that by piecing together the children's life stories and the list of possible behaviours (featured in Chapter 9) it was almost possible to work out when they were most vulnerable and when the gaps in their parenting occurred and I was thus able to deduce the kind of input they needed from me to fill these gaps. This process was not, of course, exact and so I included everything I could think of to compensate for this.

My understanding is that, providing there is no disruption through pain, illness or excessive noise to the developing foetus during its critical stages of development, the foetus will develop normally and the brain will become properly wired. This wiring continues after birth and is then dependent on how the mother/primary care-giver relates to his/her baby for how effective the wiring is.

Stages of child development

Normal development age 0–1

The baby starts to learn and develop feelings, such as feeling safe and learning to trust. This forms the basic foundation for ongoing attachment between the mother (in particular) and the father or primary care-giver. This will help the baby with the development of things like muscle control, emotions and speech development.

DISRUPTED DEVELOPMENT

If the baby's needs fail to be met for whatever reason then the baby's development may be slower than 'normal'. This can affect all the areas above – speech, muscle control, trust issues – and the baby may be unable to identify her own needs and get them met.

Normal development age 1–3

The toddler needs her primary care-giver to provide a secure base for her to explore from. Her sense of independence grows as she becomes more confident. She stands, walks, picks up small objects and is generally fascinated by everything. She will start trying to take some control over her actions and will get frustrated when she fails.

DISRUPTED DEVELOPMENT

Failure to meet these needs may result in lack of trust in the principal care-givers and she may become clingy and dependent and afraid of exploring, or become far too independent of adults and try and parent herself. This can result in regressive rather than forward-moving development.

Normal development age 3–6

She will really discover the world around her, becoming more self-reliant, dressing herself and be potty-trained. Her language will improve and she will be using her imagination, be constantly questioning and keen to learn. She will start enjoying social interaction with other children and adults and generally become more daring.

DISRUPTED DEVELOPMENT

Conversely, she may suffer feelings of guilt, blame and 'badness' and have nightmares and night traumas because of what has happened to her. She may become restless, be aggressive or be extremely clingy. She may lack coordination, have delayed language and lack curiosity.

Normal development age 6–10

She learns to understand and take control of life outside of the family, developing a picture of the world, time and space. She starts developing a conscience, sorting right from wrong, expands her reasoning and physical skills, and starts to model the significant people in her life.

DISRUPTED DEVELOPMENT

If her needs are not being met she may lack energy and be overcome with a sense of grief, feel depressed, angry and guilty, become withdrawn and overwhelmed by questions like, 'Why me? Why did this happen?' She may become bossy, do badly at school and live in a fantasy land caught up in 'magical' thinking.

Normal development age 10–16

She will experience physical changes as she enters puberty and will learn to deal with strong emotional and sexual feelings, making sense of herself and her existence in the world. She will assert herself, become independent and form friendships outside of the family. She will start questioning adult values and form her own opinions and views.

DISRUPTED DEVELOPMENT

If her needs haven't been met she may feel insecure, lack self-esteem and confidence, be confused by her own identity and experience intensifying of her emotions. She may start challenging authority and mistrust adults, get in with the wrong crowd and be easily influenced into stealing, truancy, early sexual activity, start drinking alcohol and/or taking drugs.

As mentioned, no two babies will develop in exactly the same way or in the same time-frame. It is generally accepted that they will acquire a certain skill within a 'certain range'. Likewise, the child who has experienced gaps in her parenting will not react in an exact, easily defined, easy-to-read way. There is a school of thought that says that the way we think can have a detrimental effect on our health, whereas positive thoughts lead to increased serotonin levels (the happy chemical). If the child has been fully nurtured in the first stages of her life, this will occur naturally and the brain will be properly wired. If it hasn't, the good news is that the child can still learn and the brain can subsequently be wired correctly.

From about the age of seven, children will start modelling significant people in their lives. Looking back at my own childhood, I was able to see that this was true for me. Now having had my own children for some seven years, I am in a position to confirm this as the boys have definitely worked out that our values and integrity are sound and that they have adopted them as their own.

We believe our brains are like massive computers capable of more than we know, and like a computer our brains can be reprogrammed and the software can be changed (hence the wiring can still occur for those children who suffered trauma). But it doesn't matter how much we teach, reason with or shout at the *conscious* mind, change to our 'core beliefs' can only happen in the *unconscious* mind. Most of the significant experiences that shape our thinking happen before the age of seven, and from then on we distort, generalize and only hear reinforcements of those experiences through our 'selective hearing' (explained later in this chapter) so it can become an even bigger problem in later years.

Having all this information, I started looking for ways of relating this to the boys and considering how best it could be used in their development. It is obviously up to you how technical you get here. I talked through how the brain starts to develop soon after conception whilst in the mother's tummy and how it doesn't develop fully by birth as the baby's head would be too big to get down the birth canal. It is for this reason only that the baby is born at this point; ideally it would be better if the baby stayed in the womb for another two or three months and this is why a newborn baby does very little apart from sleep for the first three months. You have to decide how much information you want to give at this point. My kids already knew quite a bit about sex and the body by this stage as I had purposely bought a children's reference book about the human body. They had already queried how a baby could get down such a thin tube. I have to say that by remaining calm, acknowledging any embarrassment and then emphasizing how incredible nature is, they have been able to take this sort of information on board in a very positive, matter of fact way.

Brain wiring

To illustrate how the brain works, I took to pen and paper and drew a diagram showing them (in a way I thought they might understand) the analogy of what the neurological wires and signals might look like in a positively developed child. Please note that I am not an expert in this field nor am I an artist! In fact I have no idea what a properly wired brain might look like other than it is apparently supposed to look rather like a tree, with the wires being represented by its branches. The wires are similar in appearance to blood vessels and the brain sends its signals/instructions to all parts of the body via these branches. So for example if you want to have a drink, your brain sends a signal to your fingers, hand and the muscles in the arm which tells them how to pick up your glass and lift it towards your mouth. The brain then sends another set of signals to your lips and mouth which tells them how to take a sip, taste the drink and swallow. Of course most of this process happens unconsciously, requiring little thought or effort.

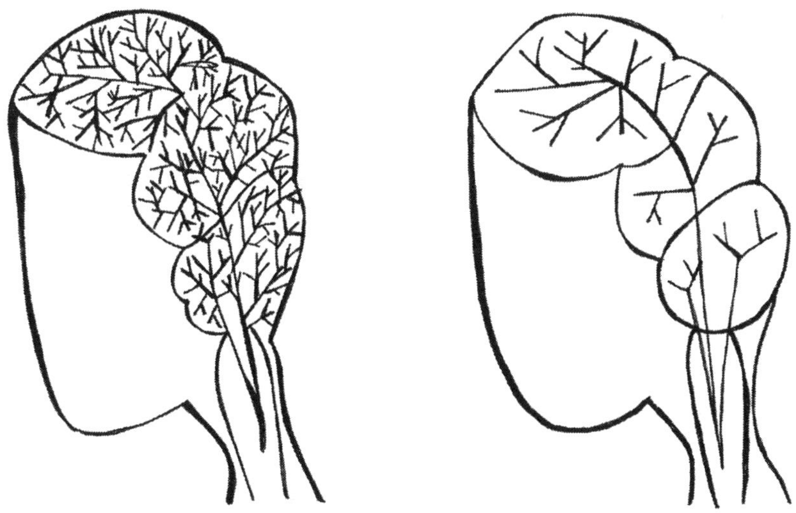

Sketch of what a properly wired brain might look like

Sketch of what a poorly wired brain might look like

Figure 6.1: Brain wiring

The idea here is to demonstrate the differences between a positively developed child's brain, and how it functions, and the brain of a child who has had interrupted development, which is what I drew next. Obviously this tree is not properly formed, so only some of the messages will get through or be confused. I told them that this is why, for example, on a hot summer's day I will find the radiator on full blast in Luke's bedroom and him walking round in a fleece, and conversely on a cold winter's day he walks around in a tee shirt, and why Adam gets into a state of panic each time he receives an instruction, instead of staying calm and listening. The idea here is to create a bit of pain and anxiety as this will lead to them wanting to do it/change themselves. Our boys were quite worried at this point and quickly asked if there was anything that can be done about all this. In return I quickly assured them with the good news that all of this can be rectified, and although there was no 'quick fix' Dad and I did have a few tricks up our sleeves that we would start implementing straight away which would make life easier for them.

For rewiring to occur, it is imperative at this point that you get your child's full cooperation as she needs to have both a psychological and a dependency shift away from using her own judgments and initial instincts to trusting and relying on yours by looking to you for guidance. To do this she needs to allow herself to become vulnerable and she will not be able to do this on her own, so will need lots of support from you. In order to rewire her disordered nervous system effectively, she needs to recognize and agree that the lack of adequate parenting she experienced and the gaps incurred are affecting her wellbeing and resulting in bad and/or inappropriate behaviour. This is bad enough in the home environment now, but if it develops further it could lead potentially to all sorts of problems when she enters into society at a later age and may also have a detrimental effect on her mental and physical health.

To get their commitment I gave the children as long as they wanted to think about this. I was pleased to find that almost immediately they both said that they wanted to do whatever was necessary. To cement this I asked them if they were absolutely sure and also told them they needed to start by admitting that they were scared of changing, trusting and allowing themselves to be vulnerable. Next I explained about the conscious and the unconscious brain, in that the conscious brain takes care of everything that we know about and everything that we are aware of, our thoughts and what we learn. The unconscious brain takes care of everything that we are unaware of, for example our body functions. The unconscious loves to take care of us, wants to please and be right. In other words, it will do whatever it thinks is right in order to protect us and will unconsciously develop ways for us to cope when under stress.

The wall round your heart

I learned about this concept from a therapist we consulted once. As unfortunately we weren't in the 'right' area, we were unable to get funding from social services, and as money was tight for us at that time we were unable to continue with him, though we were lucky enough to attend a training session run by him. Not content with just using this concept as it was, I then thought about how best to use it in conjunction with the message that we wanted to put to the boys.

When you were hurt emotionally, you started to build a wall around your heart as a way of protecting yourselves from being hurt again. This was done by your unconscious brain automatically (as I just mentioned the unconscious brain will do what it thinks is right in order to protect you). The more often this happened and the bigger the hurt, the more your 'selective hearing' heard to enforce that hurt, the more bricks you used, and the thicker/stronger/higher your protective wall got. So much so that eventually the wall was so high and thick that you stopped allowing yourself from feeling anything at all. In one sense this is good, as it protected you when really bad stuff was happening to you and you can therefore give yourself a pat on your back for being so clever that you provided yourself with that protection when you needed it.

Unfortunately what the brain doesn't automatically do (it needs some kind of intervention) is stop providing the protection when it is no longer needed. So now that all the bad stuff has stopped happening and you are safe, you don't need the protection of the wall any more.

I asked them if they felt loved and cared for and if all their needs were/are being met. I then suggested that perhaps they might like to start experiencing what being in love was like by taking down/letting go of the bricks. I explained that this might be hard as taking down the bricks means that you have to do the very thing that had you put them up in the first place, in that you have to allow yourselves to be completely vulnerable and trust your mum and dad, when your only experience of trusting adults was that they let you down.

To enforce this further I asked if Linda and Tony ever knew or ever did anything like this kind of work with them and of course they said they didn't. I then pointed out that few people know of the things that we were teaching them and asked if we would bother to teach them such things and leave them with the kind of feelings that we had on previous exercises if all we wanted to do was cause them harm now. We then shared one of those tender moments when the boys told me that they already loved me and said that they knew they could trust me, that they knew I wasn't going to let them down and most importantly they agreed that they would allow themselves to be vulnerable with Dad and me. I in turn quickly assured them that there was no way I was going to let them down as I loved them more than I ever thought possible.

To show them that I meant what I said, I quickly moved on because I wanted to give them some more good feelings. I started by telling them that I had some good news for them, that I'd recently been on a course and that I learned that they were NORMAL. What? You asked. Yes, NORMAL! Given everything that they have been through – the suffering, the abuse, the neglect, the lack of or gaps in parenting and being taken into care – they behave completely normally. Another way of looking at it might be: if you had experienced the same things your child did and had similar gaps in your learning, you may well find yourself behaving in exactly the same way they do (and you're normal, right?). They behave the way they do because they have missed out on some of the vital life lessons that a responsible mother would teach instinctively. In other words they are normal; it is their *behaviour* that is not normal. Our children are behaving in the only way they know to behave and think is right. They are therefore *doing the best that they can.* Having pointed this out to the boys, they were quite open to the idea that they now needed to learn new ways of behaving and being.

All babies are born equal

Next I was able to explain that what a child learns instinctively in its first two to three years forms her 'core beliefs' and instincts. I asked them if a child had been parented properly what they thought these instincts might be like and then what the instincts and beliefs of a poorly parented child might be like. It is these latter instincts that they will naturally fall back on and breaking this pattern takes a lot of effort and patience from all parts. I will cover this in more detail later. As a way of explaining this I filled a piece of paper with drawings of lots of babies in all shapes and sizes.

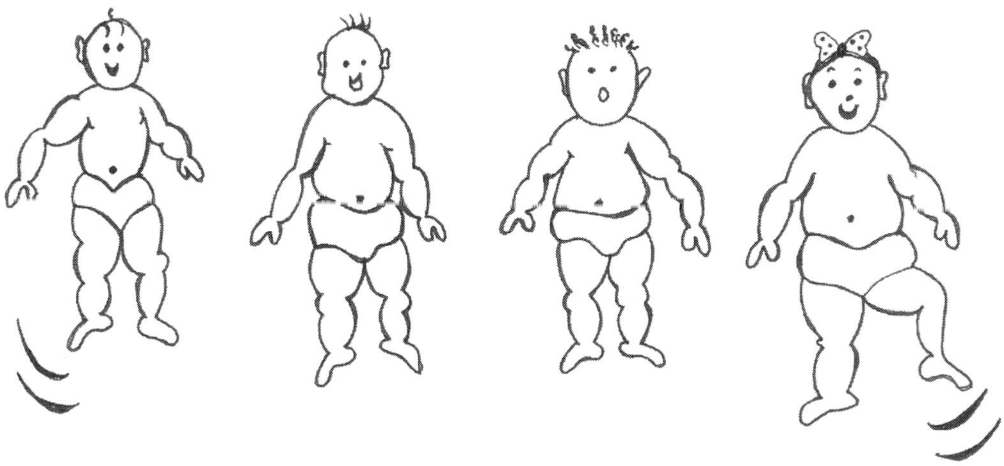

Figure 6.2: All babies are born equal

I then asked them what skills a baby is born with. We decided that she can't do very much except sleep, drink milk, burp, wee, poo and cry. In fact a newborn baby is completely innocent, helpless and reliant on its mother for everything. I asked if they thought the baby knew its name or its mum's name or knew where she was, or could tell jokes, and of course they agreed it couldn't. Therefore we can deduce that a baby is born knowing nothing and that what she can do is probably instinctive rather than learned. I then asked them, if that were the case, is it fair to say that it's what happens to that baby next that shapes her life? I got agreement for this too. So we can therefore say that whatever happens is not the baby's fault as it is the mother's responsibility to look after the baby and do a good job. Referring to the drawing of babies I asked, 'So which baby is the best? Which baby has the best chance in life? What happens if the baby has a great mum and does all the things she should and looks after and loves the baby, how will the baby grow up then?' (The penny is beginning to drop now.) 'And what happens if the mum doesn't do her job properly (for whatever reason), how will the baby grow up then?' 'Like us', was the resounding reply.

So therefore we can make the following 'distinctions' based on the things that happened to you:

- YOU ARE NOT TO BLAME.
- IT'S NOT YOUR FAULT.
- ALL BABIES ARE BORN EQUAL.
- THERE IS NO SUCH THING AS A BAD BABY.
- THERE IS NO SUCH THING AS A BAD CHILD.
- HUMAN BEINGS ARE AMAZING.
- YOU ARE AMAZING!

There is a kind of 'gobsmacked' look of realization that comes over a person when they have been incredibly stuck for a very long time and then experience a complete change to one of their 'core beliefs'. This almost 'falling off their chair in disbelief' look means that they have finally 'got it'. What is great about it is that once it has happened and the 'core belief' has been changed, it is impossible then to forget it, go back to the old way of thinking, or to do anything else other than to experience life, through the new 'core belief'. The list of statements above need to be put on the wall in big bold letters. Our children need to be reminded of them every day.

The object of telling your child all this is to create within her the desire to change. Quite simply, if you don't tell her, she may get there eventually and work things out for herself, but it will probably take a very long time, a lot of pain and sacrifice on her part as well as yours, and could well wear you both out. Or there is the strong possibility that she will never work it out at all. I am sure that you, like Chris and I, are aware that there are many 'screwed up' adults around today, which made us determined that we were going to sort our children out and get them as straight as they could be, as soon as possible, preferably before puberty started to set in. We decided that it didn't matter how much we wanted them to change, or what we did to make that happen, unless we created the desire within them to want to change themselves, then nothing would really work.

Another thing I want to include here, as I have been writing about making the children feel good, is that one day Luke had been playing up and for the millionth time I had sat down with him and helped him work something out. He asked me why I kept bothering. My reply was, 'Because I think you are worth it'. It was another of those 'gobsmacked' moments; he had never considered that this could be true or that anyone might think this about him. Since then I have included this and similar statements into my everyday conversation as often as I can. Other favourites are: 'Because I believe in you', 'Because I believe you can do it', 'Because I know you are bigger than that', and 'Because I know you can do better than that'.

As I didn't have all this information available to me in the beginning, it was in our experience really hard to define exactly what the boys had missed out on. We felt sure that they were parented some of the time, but that that parenting had been inconsistent. So we incorporated into our day-to-day lives everything we could think of (just in case) and in no particular order (more from ignorance than choice). Instinctively I gave them lots of 'mum games' and 'mum time', taking every opportunity I could to bond with them and show them how much I loved them through physical contact, silly songs and verses. I invented lots of facial games which of course involved a lot of eye contact and holding them in my arms, or sitting them on my knee, and I paid lots of attention to even the slightest little cut or bruise, kissing an area of their skin just away from the hurt then blowing the kiss towards the hurt saying, 'It will start to get better now'.

At every opportunity I treated them like little babies even to the extent of feeding them from a baby's bottle that a friend left at my house. I was amazed when they first wanted to be fed with this and I have to admit that, not realizing, I treated it as a bit of a game. However, much later I learned that this is an essential part of bonding and helps massively in the healing process of badly parented children. Had I known back then I would have treated it more seriously and put more effort into it. Luckily I did sit them on my knee and share the kind of intimacy that only a mother and child share. I guess that somewhere deep down I realized that this was the kind of attention the boys needed at that time. So rather than make a big deal of it I just left the bottle hanging around the kitchen so they could ask me when they wanted to use it. Much later a friend told me that when she learned about the importance of feeding an older adopted child (her daughter was nine at the time) in this way, she gave her daughter a bottle of milk each night and had done so for two years.

Games that encourage bonding and trust

There are lots of little games you can play with your children that will encourage bonding and trust and go a long way towards rewiring the brain, as it is often just repetition of movements and sensations that is needed for this to occur. You could try the following:

- Put the child in a blanket and swing her (two pairs of hands are better than one in this instance).
- Use swinging and rocking movements.
- Blindfold her and lead her safely round the house and garden. Then put her in the position of trust and allow her to do the same to you.
- Let her fall backwards and you catch her.
- Sit her on your knee and rock and mother her, whilst giving lots of eye contact.
- Sit her on your knee, sing nursery rhymes; I found to my horror that our children knew very few nursery rhymes, even at the ages of seven and five.
- Go swimming together, which is great if they can't already swim as they suddenly realize that they really do need you and they will cling on to you.
- Paint each other's faces.
- Bounce together on a trampoline.

For general development and bonding:

- Let them play with water and slosh water about.
- Play with play dough.
- Make stories and cartoons together.
- Play with them and their toys.
- Paint together.
- Sewing and knitting.
- Craft work and modelling.
- Gardening and sowing seeds.
- Make treasure hunts for them.
- Build houses and tents out of furniture, cushions, sheets and boxes.
- Make obstacle courses for them in the garden.
- Play Chinese whispers.

Please note that there are therapists who specialize in the area of rewiring the brain.

The longer your child is with you, the more she will start to trust you, as you keep providing for her and being there for her. We frequently drew the boys' attention to the initial promises that we made to them (we literally used to take them over to the list and point each promise out one by one). 'Do you realize you have been with us for six weeks and five days? Have we kept our promises to you? Have we fed you? Kept you safe? Have we ever let you down?' etc. By frequently emphasizing this, it allows the child to internalize the information that they are being cared for at both a conscious and an unconscious level, which in turn will speed the rate in having them trust you.

Distinctions

Next I introduced the boys to the concept of 'distinctions' and explained the following. When a child is learning to ride a bike, one of her parents will probably hold the back of the seat while the child gets the hang of it. It may take many attempts, and probably the child will fall off a few times, but with perseverance the child will eventually master it, and in the first moment when she rides the bike unassisted, she will learn the distinction of 'balance'. Once that distinction is learned, she cannot unlearn it. The same could be said for swimming. Muscles have great memories and once they learn how to do something they know how to do it for ever. Another example is the distinction 'snow'. If you think about snow, you could probably think of four or five types of snow. There are those big fluffy flakes that stick and are great for snowball fights and building snowmen. There are the small, wet flakes that land on the floor and immediately dissolve away to nothing. There is the really hard frozen type which occurs after a very cold night and then there is the damp slushy type when it starts to melt. It is interesting to know then that Eskimos, living in the climate that they do, have around 30 different distinctions for the word snow. For example, they have snow for cooking with and another kind for building with, etc.

What is great about distinctions is that once they are learned, they become second nature because they are easy to remember and in fact require no effort at all. They actually cannot be forgotten, so you will start to see changes in the way your child conducts herself and her behaviour and this will occur naturally. By using words that your children are probably unfamiliar with, they will stand out when you use them in your everyday conversations. They will therefore, once introduced, have a very deep and profound meaning. To cement what we are saying we always have a dictionary to hand when explaining new distinctions. This has several benefits in that they get to hear the true meaning of words, they get practice in looking words up, and perhaps most importantly they get to see that these words and meanings actually do exist and that you are not just making this stuff up. Introducing distinctions gives you a new framework to start working from, which will start to alleviate the pressure on you and will have a massive effect on your child as distinctions are so different to what they are used to.

Reframing

Have a good look at this, without reading further. What do you see?

Figure 6.3: Optical illusion

Do you see some black shapes on the page or do you see the word LIFE? If you didn't see the word 'life' straight away, then this is a good example of how we are 'conditioned'. Normally the background would be in white and the letters in black; that is what is normal to us, that is what we are used to. This exercise can show us that we go around in life expecting everything to be a certain way, because that is what we have learned, that is how we are 'conditioned'. This is also a good analogy of how we see life generally. Do you always see it in one way? Is it always black and white? Or is there perhaps a different way of seeing it? Another example of how we are 'conditioned' is when you go through a doorway and bang your arm. There is no reason for this other than your mind has equated that you are going through a doorway. Heaven knows how many doorways you've been through in your life, but you bang your arm because your brain isn't seeing the doorway that you are walking through now; it just knows that it is walking through a doorway and it is remembering a previous doorway.

Knowing that we are 'conditioned' to think in a certain way – always to expect, based on what has happened before – is very useful, as once we know that this is how our brains naturally operate, we can then use 'reframing' to alter our child's thinking. We can prevent their thoughts becoming imbedded in their subconscious, creating new problems for their unconscious brains to solve, and also we can alter both the 'conditioned responses' (see Chapter 7) they already have and also our own. Our 'conditioned responses' are based on the negatives that we have learned in life. So, for example, something happens:

- As a result of that your brain decides that you are bad.
- From then on your brain will look for other ways to enforce the idea that you are bad; which is 'selective hearing'. It doesn't matter how many good things it now hears, your brain has decided that you are bad and will only hear those enforcements that it now wants to hear, as your brain likes to be 'right' and was 'right' to make that decision.
- The brain is now 'stuck' in this pattern of thinking, possibly for ever.
- Our brain then responds to life as it happens through this 'conditioned response'. It is similar to wearing tinted glasses: once you have put them on, you have to see the world and how it occurs through that tint.

The brain not only likes to be right, it also likes to do whatever it can to protect you. A really good example of this is that there are many large women around who, if they were to get to the bottom of their weight problem, would find that their brains had decided to make them overweight to protect them after they have been put down or shocked in some way about their femininity, their sexuality, their ability to function in a man's world, etc. Once the underlying issue is discovered and acknowledged, it is then usually possible to reprogramme the brain to think differently and therefore resolve the issue by doing whatever it needs to do to rectify the problem.

'Reframing' is merely seeing things from a different point of view. So often we get so stuck in our 'conditioned responses' that we can only see things in a certain way, but by recognizing this and opening up our minds we are then able to see things differently and put things into a different context. In a lot of respects, this book is based on this ideal. To have our children accept what has happened to them, learn from the experience and move on, we need to change their 'conditioned responses' by reframing their experiences and putting them into a new context. The better you become at this, the more you teach your child and the more she understands this, the easier she will find it to change her responses and subsequently the way she behaves. So, for example, by putting things into a different context by reframing, you can show your child that their feelings of being 'bad' are just a 'conditioned response'.

Throwing a different light on to what happened to her and allowing her to see it in a different way will enable her to rewrite the history of her life in a more powerful and satisfactory way. For example, having learned of this, my boys said that they are actually quite glad that all that stuff happened to them because it eventually brought them to us and that they are happy now. (Please note that they said this of their own volition.) When I asked them how they could use the experience of what happened to them and 'reframe' it to make them more powerful, they replied that they could use it to feel stronger. After all, if they survived all that, they must be pretty strong and they did, so they are!

The loving cup

At bath time we used a different plastic cup to represent each of the boys and two plastic jugs to represent Chris and me. Then, making sure they were empty, we covered each cup with cling film. We showed them how much water each jug held, that there was plenty there and told them the water represented the amount of love that Dad and I had. We showed them that in our relationship if one of us had a hard day and lost some of our water and started to feel unloved, then the other would come along, talk about what had happened thus making the other feel better and loved by filling their jug up. We then demonstrated what we meant a couple of times by pouring water from one jug to another and threw in a couple of kisses and thanked each other, for good measure.

Then we told them to hold their cups up. We asked them how much love was in their cups and they answered, 'None', because they had put up barriers (cling film) and didn't let the love in. We then showed them what it was like when we tried to pour our love into them. Of course because of the cling film the water poured away and they were left feeling empty, or deprived of love. We asked them what they needed to do to feel loved and they said they needed to make a hole in the cling film to let the water in. We asked them what that really meant and they agreed that they needed to start trusting us by taking down the barriers and by talking about their problems. We then made a small hole in the cling film and showed them what receiving just a little love would be like and then they completely broke the cling film and allowed their cups to be filled with love. We then told them that by allowing love in, they would soon find that they were able to give love out, by filling our jugs and that was what it was like to be in a normal, healthy family relationship.

Chapter 7

Family History

We felt right from the start that our children needed to hear the truth about what had happened to them and why they had been taken into care. Unfortunately this was complicated in our case by the fact that Linda contested the adoption. It was therefore very difficult to know how best to relate their story to them, given that we didn't know the expected ending. We found that social services were reluctant to do anything either, and they advised us not to tell the children that they might not be staying with us after all, and so we were all left in a state of limbo. We felt awful about this as, on the one hand, they obviously needed to hear the truth about their past – and we could see very clearly the difference that would have made to them – and, on the other, had we told them the truth they would then have had to live with the uncertainty of their future with us.

It wasn't until they had been with us for two years, and the adoption had gone through, that they actually got to hear their 'life story', although I had kept the idea alive with a photo album, a family tree and as much 'safe' information as possible, in order to address their needs to know where they had come from. Social services had been very helpful and made the relevant files available to us and even collated their story for us. I have heard several people say that they were advised not to say anything derogatory about the birth parents to their children. The trouble with this advice is that the child then tends to put the birth parents on a pedestal, fantasize about the 'perfect life' that they had, often using it to manipulate you, whilst suspecting you of being a liar. You surely know the truth, and know that they know the truth too, but you are letting them get the better of you because you are not correcting them, so then you have another set of issues to deal with.

Telling them the truth

With all this in mind, we felt there had to be a happy medium. I truly believe that anyone who knowingly hurts another person must be so 'conditioned', (probably as they themselves have suffered) as to think that their behaviour is normal and therefore acceptable. Therefore I think that there has to be a balance when talking about our children's birth parents which neither puts them on a pedestal nor puts them down without explanation. I have found that it is better to tell the truth gently, as we know it from the files, let the children draw their own conclusions and then 'reframe' that view for them by putting it into the context just mentioned.

For us it seemed obvious that the children needed to hear the truth, but also their birth parents would benefit from being told the truth. No one can begin the healing process if they don't understand what they are healing from. We felt this was especially true for Linda, in that she needed to be told that the children were taken away because she didn't do a good enough job as a parent and that the children needed to have therapy, not to deal with their separation from her (as she seemed to think) but to deal with the problems that had arisen for them as a result of poor parenting and being taken into care in the first place. Of course this didn't happen; she was never told.

Birth parents need to be told the truth in this rather blunt, non-judgmental way so that:

- They 'get it'.
- They understand where the children are at and possibly why they no longer want to see them.
- By hearing the truth, they can finally internalize it, deal with it, take responsibility for it and move on.
- They can understand that the child is having therapy not because of anything that is happening to them now.
- They then need to hear that you are working with the child towards forgiveness on their part.

It's a bit like going to the doctor's if you feel ill, but are not sure what is wrong with you. Until you actually see the doctor you may imagine all sorts of things: you may imagine the worst, but it is not till you actually go to the doctor, have the tests, then hear the diagnosis and you know the truth about what is happening, that you can deal with it in whatever way you need to deal with it, accept it, have any necessary treatment and then start to heal and move on. (It's getting to be a familiar process isn't it!)

Therapy

When we adopted the boys, it was agreed by the court that social services should fund assessments and any subsequent therapy needed to get the boys straight. It is always advisable to have this built into the adoption agreement, even if you are adopting a baby or child who seems to be perfectly normal and unaffected, as who knows what reactions they may suffer later on. I have heard of several children adopted as babies having post traumatic stress disorder much later. At first, we found it quite difficult to convince the 'powers that be' that there was a need for therapy. This was because to all intents and purposes the boys were outwardly well-behaved and charming. We were only successful in this when the court assigned a second Guardian Ad Litum to write an assessment for them for consideration in the final process of adoption.

Chris and I were very clear as to the type of therapist we wanted for Luke. We guessed that as social services have limited funds, and we certainly didn't want to waste them, we were probably only going to get one stab at this, so it was imperative that we got it right first time by finding the right person. Luke needed someone very strong who dared to be intrusive, who was prepared to have one of us present at every session and who was prepared to educate Chris and me in order to understand Luke's condition and then to advise us how best to deal with it. This therapist was extremely hard to find, as probably the most important criterion was that he/she needed to understand Luke and his condition. We both had to remain adamant that we were not going to be fobbed off with just any therapist and strong that to have the wrong therapist could cause more harm than good.

We felt totally justified with this when we did eventually find the right person and Luke was assessed as having a dissociative disorder.

There are numerous overlapping forms of this condition, and further information can be found on the MIND and NAMI websites, for example. Our understanding is that this condition can affect certain people when faced with a traumatic event. The person develops a specific 'personality' as a way of coping with that particular trauma, and the more ongoing, severe and the more traumas incurred the more personalities that person can develop as a way of coping with each of those events.

My interpretation of the reality of living with someone with this condition is that it is like living with several completely different people inside one body, with each person having his own personality, likes and dislikes and level of understanding and intellectual ability. Each personality does not know that the other exists and there is no recollection of any 'conversations' taking place between the different personalities, although these can happen. I am sure you will comprehend the difficulties we incurred trying to understand this condition and the frustration we experienced living with this on a day-to-day basis, never knowing, literally from moment to moment, which personality we were talking to and dealing with, and at its simplest level not knowing if the personality sitting at the dinner table was the one that liked peas or not. Through therapy we did, however, come to understand each of Luke's personalities, where they came from, their likes and dislikes and their needs, and more importantly how to deal with his condition when something triggered him to fragment in this way, how to bring him out of these personalities and have Luke take control again and learn for himself how to cope with this.

It is important to point out that although Chris and I consider ourselves to be pretty insightful when it comes to the boys, and in fact human behaviour generally, I have to say that there is no way on earth we would ever have worked out the way Luke's mind operated without meeting his therapist, let alone know how to sort him out. I would also say at this point that although Luke dominates this book, it is the part of Luke that I have seen duplicated in many adopted children that I write about. Other than the description above, I have made no attempt to write about the part of Luke that needed therapy, beyond that of other adopted children, as I prefer to leave that to the experts.

It can be both a benefit and a nuisance having your child 'labelled'. A label often leads to interpretation and therefore people tend to treat your child in a certain way. However, for us (and I know the same is true for many other people I have met) it has served as a blessing to have an explanation as to why our child was behaving in the way that he did. Also for us it confirmed that we weren't going mad ourselves, as to all extents and purposes, until you really got to know him, Luke was outwardly quite well-behaved and charming and most people didn't see or understand the extent of his odd behaviour at home, which for the most part was directed at me.

Having the diagnosis and then understanding how and why he behaves the way he does was extremely useful as not only did we come to understand his problem ourselves but we were then able to educate his teachers, to the extent that we wrote lists of 'user instructions', so that if he did 'x' it would benefit him if they responded with 'y'. This was great as he was then receiving continuity of responses from his therapist, his school and also at home. Unfortunately I have to say that we found some teachers a lot more cooperative than others, so with his school work, in some years he flourished and in others he seemed to be constantly in trouble. I have never understood the sense in telling someone that their child is annoying! In my opinion each child is doing the best that they can or know how to, given their circumstances and experiences of life; if their behaviour doesn't fit with the expected norm, there will be a reason for this. I must add, though, that having such a diagnosis can be dangerous. There are plenty of support groups out there for all sorts of conditions. Whereas it is great to learn the 'how's and 'why's, and learn how to handle someone with a condition, and in Luke's case how he actually processed information and how his brain worked, in my opinion some support groups support you to keep on having those symptoms. It is my firm belief that where possible the child/person would be better if they learned what they need to learn, that we help them to come to terms with their condition, support the child/person whilst they learn to handle their condition, and then allow them to move on and grow.

We had Adam assessed by Luke's therapist too and she suggested that he have a course of play therapy, as he seemed to have dealt with his trauma in a more efficient way. Although we weren't sure how effective this would turn out to be, we felt that it did benefit him/us as we now had a third party to tell him his life story. He says that his therapy helped him to learn how to play better, but when I asked if it helped to sort out his past, he said that apart from hearing his life story, no. It did, however, serve to have him not feel 'left out', as Luke needed or seemed to be getting a lot of attention through the massive amount of time he spent in therapy, and also gave Chris and I some more ideas. We now know/feel that Adam was just too young and wasn't ready or able to face up to dealing with his issues.

Life is like a book

Adam told me recently that it really helped when we suggested to the boys that they think of their life like a book with lots of different chapters. We split it up for them like this:

Chapter 1 Being born and living with Linda up to the night they were taken into care.

Chapter 2 The children's first foster homes and being reunited.

Chapter 3 Living with their second foster family.

Chapter 4 Moving in with us.

Chapter 5 Moving house together and starting and settling into secondary school.

This exercise helped them to see:

- that just like a book, which they could pick up when they wanted, take a look, then close and put down or leave on the book shelf, they could do the same with their past, until such time when they felt strong enough to look at it objectively; so they didn't actually have to carry the book or the 'baggage' around with them all the time
- that all the really awful stuff happened in the first chapter and that since then their lives have started to get better
- that just like the book, their lives have barely just begun and there are plenty more chapters to read and write and they can choose the tone of the rest of the book for themselves

- that the authors of the book (birth parents, foster parents and then adoptive parents) have changed and they are really happy with the present authors.

The purpose of telling the child their life story is to match the 'truth' with the 'pictures' in their heads. By confronting the 'truth', it then frees them up to deal with it, by getting angry, depressed, tearful, violent (whatever they need to do and feel), accept it and then move on. It is for this reason that the earlier this is dealt with the better. Discussing this with both of the boys' therapists we agreed that it would be far better and more effective if the boys heard their life story from their therapists as a third party. We used our therapists for this, but it would have been equally effective if a social worker had done it, or it would also probably have worked if a social worker was seen to deliver a file to the house, as it makes it more credible when it comes from a third party and stops the child taking it out on you, if they don't like what they hear.

Adam's therapist wrote a similar, personalized synopsis for both boys, which was duly read to each of them separately. It was fairly matter of fact and included a lot of the stuff that they so badly needed to hear. Neither boy seemed surprised. In fact they were both pretty accepting of it and if anything they said it did match with their images of the past and explained a lot. I went over their stories again with them on my own the next day, this time getting out our files too and adding a few more bits that I thought were really relevant. I wanted them to know, understand and really take on board that they were not taken into care as a result of that one day when Linda fell 'asleep' on the settee and that it wasn't because Luke put a blanket over her encouraging her to 'sleep', but that they had been taken into care after a long chain of events and as a result of the numerous warnings from doctors, health visitors, etc. and also many calls to social services from concerned neighbours. I also wanted them to see that each time social services received a call Linda was offered help, which she usually refused, or if she accepted the advice that was offered initially, was unable to sustain it for any period of time. I felt it was important for them to know that being taken into care wasn't because social services one day came along and decided to move them, which turned out to be pretty much what they had thought; I wanted them to know that social services weren't the 'bad guys' and I was thus able to 'reframe' completely their image of them.

I got into the habit of going over the therapist's work after each session, especially with Luke, as his sessions were often intense and covered a lot of ground. I wanted to make sure that he both understood and had digested the work and got the maximum benefit from each session. I also had him repeat everything he learned in each session to Chris as a way of cementing it further (I attended every session with Luke whilst Chris entertained Adam). I made posters for his bedroom wall, which I duly removed as he progressed in therapy to prevent him from getting stuck.

Looking at the birth parents' history

Having looked at the boys' life stories, I then asked them to consider what life must have been like for their birth parents. First, I reminded them that '*all babies are born equal*' and that '*it is what happens next*' that shapes your life. I then asked them to use the information they had learned from their life story to consider what life was like for Linda. They remembered that life hadn't been great for her and that her mum had died when she was young, so we worked out that as her mum wasn't around after the age of ten and was probably busy being ill for some time before that, and given that girls normally learn how to be a mum from their mums, there was no one from whom to learn how to be a 'proper' mum. When a woman has a baby she is supposed somehow to just know how to be a mother; she just has to get on with it. Also – and we can only guess this – Linda's mum could only teach her what she knew herself and she might not have had a great childhood herself. I also pointed out that there is no school to go to, to learn how to be a 'good' parent (the more's the pity!). Then I pointed out that Linda had been a baby once and that '*all babies are born equal*', so that means that she had been born equal too and that '*it's what happens next that shapes your life*'. Ah ha!

We then worked out that her dad didn't sound great either as he gave her a very hard time, and when he remarried, her step mum didn't treat her well either, but that they too had been babies once and they had been born equal and innocent and that the reason things went wrong for them was (again guessing) that they had not had great childhoods themselves and that their parents were lacking in parenting skills too, and so we went on. I then pointed out that there was a definite pattern to this and asked them to consider what the parents of someone who frequently beat their wives might be like. Or someone who was a criminal? Adding Tony to the equation and not knowing that much from the files about him, we could guess from the way he treated them that he too lacked some of the skills needed to be a responsible parent so we decided that he couldn't have been very responsible as he had let them down too and if he had been a more capable or responsible parent, or done things differently, they might be living with him now. I pointed out that he too had been a baby once and that he too had been born equal, but if we looked at his parents we guessed that was where he had learned to be like that, but the parents too had been babies once, etc.

Next we asked them to point out whom we should blame. Luke automatically pointed to Linda, saying that it must be her fault. 'But how can it be when she was a baby once and born equal and babies are completely innocent and learn from the people around them?' Then the finger went to her mum then to her mum's mother, then Adam pointed it at Tony, but we always answered the same. 'So what can we make from this?' we finally asked.

NO ONE IS TO BLAME!

People can only do what they can do with the resources and knowledge that they have and despite what anyone might think, *everyone is doing the best that they can. No one can teach you something if they haven't been taught how to do it themselves.* I pointed out to them that we didn't believe that Linda or Tony had woken up one day and thought to themselves, 'What can we do to make life difficult for our children?' 'They genuinely were doing the best that they knew' and yes, it was our firm belief that both their birth parents loved them dearly; they just hadn't learned the right way of expressing that love through commitment and responsibility, nor had they learned how to deal with and express their own emotions.

I then told them that none of the things that had happened to them should have happened to them and reminded them that I wished we had never had the opportunity to adopt them in the first place. 'What?' Adam cried immediately, who hadn't heard this before. 'I would have much preferred that you had had a fantastic childhood and that Linda and Tony had given you the kind of parenting that you needed. I would have much preferred that you had never been taken away from them and put into care. I hate it that all those horrible things happened to you. In fact I wish that no child ever had to go through those kinds of experiences and if that meant that we had never met you and that we had to remain childless, then so be it. At least you wouldn't have suffered. In my mind if you truly love someone that means that you only want what is best for them.' I was pleased to find that Luke remembered having had this conversation with me before. Adam's response was to throw his arms around me and sob his heart out. When he could eventually speak, he told me he was crying happy tears because he finally understood just how much I love him. He was really funny after that. Every few minutes he'd run over to me, fling his arms around me again and tell me in a deep sigh just how much he loved me. He was absolutely euphoric for at least two days!

Conditioned responses

Going back to the last exercise we decided that no one is to blame. I reminded them that it is usually in the first three years of life that we decide how the world is and form our beliefs, our basic instincts, our 'conditioned responses' and that we learn these from the people around us.

If we were to put a three-year-old in a room and then constantly shout at him and tell him that he was no good, he would grow up to be very scared, lacking confidence and have no self-worth. Responding accordingly, he would grow up to think that the world was a bad place and he would frequently miss out on the opportunities that came his way. Conversely, if we put a three-year-old child in a room and constantly told him how clever he was, praising him and showering him with love, responding accordingly he would grow up loving himself, confident and believing that the world was a good place full of opportunities. He would also believe that he was a 'good' person and capable of anything. Having said this, I reminded them that a person can only teach something that they know themselves. Linda and Tony could only teach them based on the kind of input that they had had in their early lives. I told them that each of us walks round with a three-year-old inside us. This three-year-old has already worked out how the world is, he has formed his belief system, and unless someone intervenes and manages to change these beliefs the three-year-old will not grow up, but stay three forever.

Forgiving the parents

I was then able to suggest that it might help them to think that, even though Linda and Tony are now adults, how scared the three-year-old inside of them must feel (as surely their three-year-olds hadn't had the opportunity to grow up) and to remember that they too were born equal and innocent. When you start to think of people in this way, walking around with a scared three-year-old inside of them, it is hard not to be more forgiving. I told them that if they did still find it hard to forgive them directly that they might find it easier to forgive them *for not being the kind of parents that they needed.* That does not mean that what happened to them was right or acceptable; it simply means that their birth parents needed to be forgiven for:

- not being the kind of parents that they needed – how could they be, they didn't know how
- being weak or naive and not accepting the help that was offered.

I also pointed out that it wasn't healthy to walk around holding on to a lot of pain or anger and that it is always better to look for ways of releasing those feelings, and that even if they didn't know how to do this yet, they needed at least to recognize this fact and look deep in their hearts and work towards forgiving them. For now at least it would be better to accept that they were willing to find a way to forgive them for not treating them in the way that they needed.

I then told them that no matter how hard we try, or how much we would like to, we can't change the past. Luke had often said that he had forgotten all about the past and had blocked it out. The problem with this is that, although it is possible to get very good at this, one day, when you least expect it, something will happen to remind you of the past and it will leap out and grab you and cause you to react in a strange way. You won't be able to function properly until you come to terms with and deal with what happened to you. This is why 'triggers' completely overpower and consume you, thrusting you back into memories of the past, which you thought you had forgotten. They have you fall back on those first learned 'conditioned responses'/instinctive behaviours as a way of survival, when they no longer have the same effect in your world today. The trick is to know this:

You can't forget the past, block it out or hide from it, so you need to learn to live with it and accept that what happened to you, happened to you.

Then you need to learn to avoid giving those old thoughts power by not letting them affect you any more. When you find yourself berating yourself, telling yourself that you are bad, unworthy, stupid, unloved, not good enough, too fat, too thin, too tall, too short, not as clever as your brother, or whatever other nasty thing that you might come up with, you can gently remind yourself that on the inside you have a scared little three-year-old child and he doesn't deserve to be spoken to like that. You can learn to look after him, nurture him and be much kinder to him. You can picture yourself taking hold of his hand and giving him the love that he deserves, showing, explaining and teaching him and allowing him to grow up.

What happened to you, happened back then; it is not still happening to you now. So you don't need those old thoughts and behaviours any more. You are in charge of your thoughts and beliefs now. You don't have to hold on to the limiting beliefs that others had and passed on to you. They were their beliefs about themselves. They don't serve you, so you can release them and let them go. It is time to update your beliefs and start to think differently about yourself and the world you live in now and decide and choose for yourself what you want to believe. You need to accept that you are and are always going to be all right, despite what happened to you, and that what happened to you has only served to make you a stronger person. Give yourself a huge pat on the back for surviving and stop and know that to continue having those old thoughts would be the same as giving all your power back to your old abuser, thus allowing him to still abuse you now.

The past has gone. There is nothing you can do to change that. The future hasn't come yet, so you haven't got that yet. All you have is now. You need to learn to live in the 'now' because that is all there is, and it is what you decide to do right now that will shape your future.

Amazingly the boys understood all of this and took it on board.

Breaking the pattern

Next I reminded them that there had been a definite and repeating pattern to the way they and their birth parents had been parented. We asked them what they thought they needed to do to not have the same pattern repeated with their own (future) children. They both decided that they needed to '*break the pattern*' as they definitely didn't want to hurt their children. They said they would therefore do whatever it took to be different and that they wanted us to teach them how to make them into responsible parents. We told them that it was going to take a huge amount of effort on their part as they had already had several years of living the way they had, and whenever something happens it is in our nature to fall back automatically on what we know to see us through. The thing to know is that *you are safe now* and you don't need to use those strategies or behaviours any more. They were great back then when you needed them; they protected you from what was happening then; today they are no longer needed so they either need dumping or updating to suit the life you have now. The trouble is, as Luke's therapist pointed out, that it is like the first 'language' they ever learned, so it's really hard to forget. In fact you cannot; it would be like trying to unlearn your name. So instead they have to learn a 'new' language – the language of the people who are their parents now – which will be hard because we (as human beings) always instinctively turn to our first language in times of trouble or stress. The good news is that it *is* possible, otherwise how would people learn to speak foreign languages? And everyone knows that it is much easier to learn a foreign language if you actually live in that country and hear it being spoken every day.

We decided that we should cement this information in another way so we asked them to think about what they needed to do to grow a tree, encouraging them to come up with the answers, but obviously filling in the gaps as necessary.

Find a suitable spot for your tree. You will need to consider if the tree will do best in full or partial sunlight or shade. Will it be exposed to too much wind? How much space will its roots need when it grows? What type of soil does it like? How large will it grow? Will it look good if you plant it there? Then when you have considered these things, you can move on to the actual planting:

- Dig a hole to the correct depth.
- Get the soil ready by adding manure, then water.
- Put the seedling in the hole and cover with the manure-enriched soil and water well.
- Give it all the nourishment and water it needs.
- Give it all the attention it needs by staking, to keep it straight, pruning to encourage growth, etc.

If all these considerations are met and the tree is well looked after and nourished, it will then start to establish firm roots. It is only when they are established that the tree can start to grow, and incidentally the roots will take what seems a very long time to establish underground before it starts to grow above ground. So what happens if a tree grows without strong roots? It blows over in the first strong gust of wind! The point of this is that because you weren't parented properly when you were young, your roots (or foundations) are shaky. So what we need to do now is put a stake in the soil for you to lean on, strengthen those roots by giving you nourishment and special treatment, rebuilding those foundations and then you too can grow up straight and strong.

Circles of love

Last on this subject we did one final exercise which we pinched from Adam's therapist. On a piece of paper we drew a circle and put the boys' names in it. The idea is to keep drawing larger circles, putting the names of all the people who support them. Our circles named: them, us, our family, their old family, all their foster parents and social services, the Guardian Ad Litums, the judges, friends, neighbours, the church, the school, etc. We then pointed out that there are an awful lot of people who support them and want them to do well. We put a candle on a tray to represent each of these groups of people and lit them. As the candles burned brightly we told them to think of the flames and their brightness as the love and support that all these people were sending to them and their wishes that they would now grow straight and strong.

Summary

So to recap, your child needs to be allowed to grieve and come to terms with her loss or separation. To do this she will need lots of support, empathy, patience and understanding. She needs to understand her life story (warts and all) in order for her to understand where she has come from, why she was taken into care and match the pictures of what happened with the ones in her head. (I think it is important to say here that we didn't give them every detail of what happened to them, but we did give a realistic overview.) It is then and only then that she can start to move on.

Doing the exercise on 'all babies are born equal' and looking at the history of her birth parents (even if there are a lot of guesses in there) should help her make sense of things further. She needs to know that she is worth the effort, that none of what happened should have happened, and that she is not to blame in any way. Doing all of this will massively increase her self-esteem, and it is from this point onwards that you can start to help her shape her new identity. She needs to see that she is normal and has behaved in a normal fashion, given what she had to go through. She needs to understand that she has been through a totally unusual set of circumstances and that it is this that is not normal, not her. She has suffered from poor and inconsistent parenting and whatever kind of abuse that she incurred, which means that she didn't learn all the lessons that a child would normally learn, and because of that her brain wasn't wired properly in the first place. Then she suffered from being separated from her birth parents and taken into care and subsequent moves within the care system. She needs to understand that all this has shaken her identity and now she needs to come to terms with what happened and it is all part of the normal grieving process.

Next she needs to understand that if she wasn't taught properly in the first place, she has developed poor self-image and doesn't know how to express her emotions properly. It is not surprising that she doesn't know how to behave now, and a lot of this 'bad behaviour' is her way of saying 'I don't know what to do'. She then needs your reassurance that you are going to work it out together, that you will teach her new and better behaviours, and you will teach her how to express herself properly.

There is one more analogy to illustrate this. You could think of your life as though it were a brick wall. Starting at the bottom, each brick represents a lesson that we needed to learn. If you had strong, loving, supportive parents, each lesson will have been taught and learned well, forming a strong base for the rest of the wall. If, however, some of those bricks are missing or the lessons weren't taught well, the wall will start to weaken, waiver and perhaps even fall. The trouble is that, as adoptive parents, it is hard to know which lessons were completely missed and which are just a bit shaky. So the only solution is to back track and re-teach all the lessons again. Gaining your child's commitment will go a long way to speeding up this process and a lot of this ground will be covered unconsciously by you as you attach and attune with her. Other aspects are covered in this book.

Chapter 8

Dealing with Emotions

By now your child is starting to settle. You have kept all your promises to her, and as a way of cementing your relationship have frequently brought this to her attention. She is fed and looked after each day and you are consistently meeting her needs. She has a good sense of what being a part of this family means. She is opening up to you and unconsciously beginning to recognize that she needs you. On the one hand she enjoys being with you and loves her new life, and on the other she is bombarding you with bad behaviour. Any honeymoon period you had is well and truly over. So if you have reached this stage of the process and are tearing your hair out:

CONGRATULATIONS!

You have created a safe environment for her to express her inner turmoil. She doesn't know it, and probably wouldn't admit it yet if she did, but she is beginning to trust you. She is a crazy mixed-up child who is suffering from the grief of separation and loss of her former parents and life, has loss of, or badly shaken, identity, poor self-esteem, huge gaps in both her emotional and academic learning, and an inability to recognize, let alone express, her emotions. She is now recognizing (still at an unconscious level) that she is beginning to consider her new home as home, that this time it will be for ever, and she is subsequently likening it to her birth home. She wants to recreate the atmosphere of her birth home and all that she was once familiar with in order to feel comfortable, as this is her idea of what comfortable and familiar means, or at least she knows how to 'be' in this atmosphere.

It is interesting to know that in life most of our everyday actions are generally dictated by our need and desire to seek pleasure or avoid pain. It is perhaps not surprising to find out that, for our damaged children, the opposite is true, in that they will do whatever it takes to avoid pleasure and readily welcome the things that give them pain. This is why they frequently sabotage special occasions and the treats that you give them. They often feel so 'bad' that they actually think that they don't deserve to have nice things and treats. As adoptive parents we then face the challenge of overcoming these issues so that they can live in our homes in the way that we want them to live and so that they are able to accept that they *do* deserve to have everything you want to give them and they *do* in fact deserve to have fantastic lives.

Most people don't try and 'find themselves' until they are much older. Most of us are well into adulthood before we get to deal with our 'inner issues and demons', but these traumatized children need to deal with their baggage, make sense of it all and 'find themselves' as soon as possible if they are to have a stab at normal life. Chris and I both felt that it was really important and were determined that the boys be as straightened out as they could be before the onset of puberty when we would potentially face another set of challenges. I have met many people who have said that they don't discuss their child's past with them nor do they do any work of this nature as their child seems to be all right and not have any issues. I then meet them again a year or two later and hear of all the difficulties they are then having with their child.

We found that Luke was really quite good at avoiding talking about the past and that he was able to block it out and pretend that none of it happened. In fact he preferred to do this as confronting his issues was so painful. Unfortunately though, we found that these same issues would often leap out and grab him and render him incapable of behaving acceptably. They did need to be addressed, no matter how painful. A few months after he moved in, he started playing a game where he used to put his head up inside my jumper and pretend that he was in my tummy and then that I was giving birth to him. This was all very cute and endearing, but I also recognized that, although it would be very easy to let him start believing that he was indeed my natural child, in the long term this would not do him any good. With this in mind, I assured him that I wished that this had been the case and that I had given birth to him, but sadly I knew that it wasn't and so managed to coax him into looking into the past with a sack full of reassurance and the promise that he would feel much better and indeed freer once he/we had done so.

Transposing

Your child is now transposing her feelings on to you. She gives you her feelings because she expects you to know what to do with them. She doesn't understand her emotions, let alone know how to name them, express them, or deal with them. If you're not sure what I mean by this, the telltale sign is when you suddenly find yourself feeling angry, frustrated, sad, jealous, unloved, irritated, etc. for no apparent reason. She also takes out all her anger and resentment towards her birth mother on you, as even though you are nothing like her, she is unable to differentiate between you and her in that, to her, the word 'mother' means her birth mother, but you are the 'mother' who is there, so for her you represent all 'mothers'. It is actually not meant to be personal (although it will probably feel as though it is), so reframing this with a positive light you could take this technically as a compliment that she trusts you enough to give you her feelings as she thinks you know what to do with them!

When Luke's therapist pointed out to him how he dumped all 'his stuff' on to me, he was mortified and could clearly see the effect his actions were having on me. He genuinely didn't want to hurt me. She calmly told him that he wasn't allowed to do it any more and things did start to improve, especially as, when he forgot, I quietly reminded him of this conversation and told him that, 'I don't deserve to have your "stuff" dumped on me'. I added: 'It would be much better if you just told me how you were feeling, then perhaps I might be able to help you and, if you don't know what name to give your feelings, you could just tell me that you are feeling odd, or muddled up. Then I could help you with the rest.' I was then able to explain that not being able to express his emotions properly was a good example of, and a consequence of, one of those 'life lessons' that he had missed out on. So with this in mind I made the four charts I will go on to describe below. I made one for each of us in bright colours and stuck them round the kitchen for all to see.

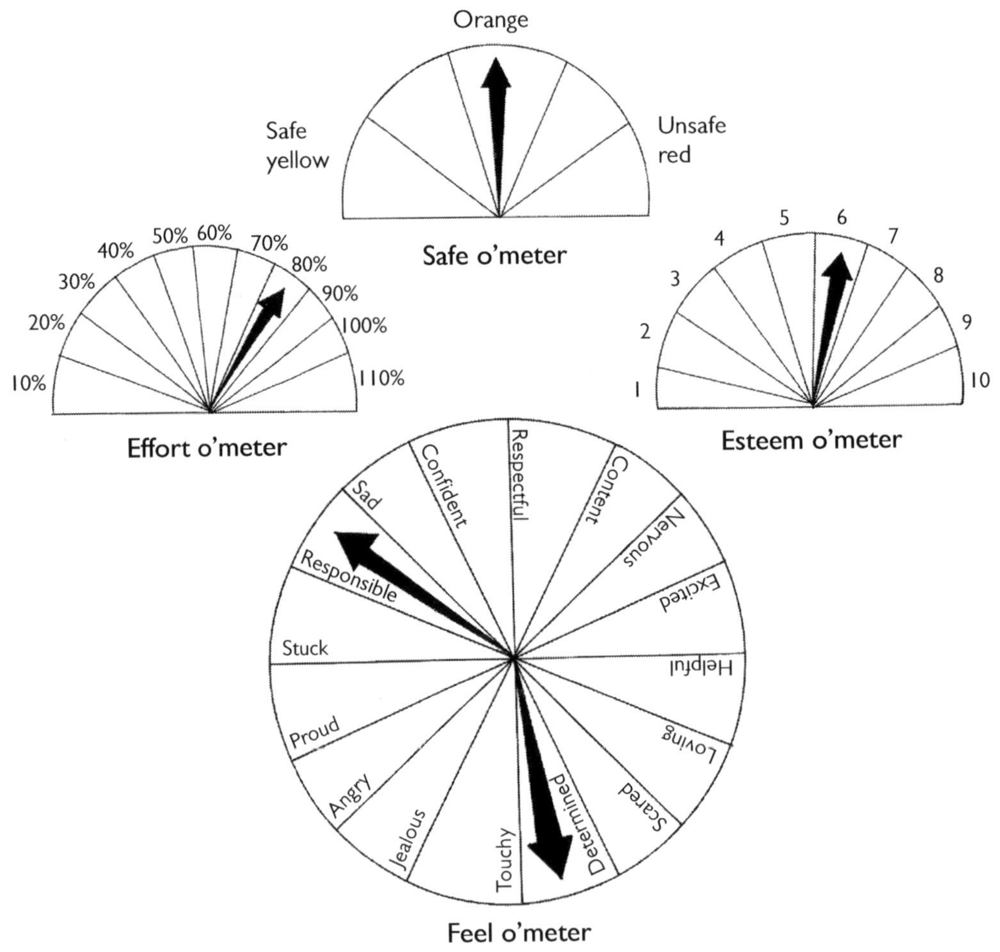

Figure 8.1: Our four charts

I invented all four charts to teach the boys about their feelings and help them make sense of the 'big muddle of string in their heads' (Luke's definition of his feelings) so that they could experience for themselves the full spectrum of their emotions, learning how to name them, verbalize them, handle them, understand the effect their feelings had on both themselves and on others, change any that they wanted to get rid of, and to understand how someone else might be feeling at any given time. With this in mind I made charts for Chris and me too.

When I first made these charts, the boys found it really hard to name more than just a few feelings. I found it really useful to have a dictionary to hand to explain the definition of new emotions to them. The dictionary also served as a 'third person' enabling them to see that these feelings really did exist and that I wasn't just making it all up. I was amazed at how quickly they got the hang of it, and it wasn't long before Luke declared that the 'piece of string' in his forehead was getting straighter! I had to add to and change the feelings on the dial several times to make them more sophisticated. The two pointers for the feel o'meter were not always enough as the boys often felt several different things at the same time. It was beneficial for them to see that it didn't matter how tired, ill, crabby or stressed Chris and I were, we were always responsible. We left one pointer permanently on 'responsible'. The emotions on the dial related to the challenges faced by each of us, so Chris's and mine were very different to the boys', and theirs also differed to allow for their individual personalities. Chris said that it helped him to focus on the day ahead as he switched his dial to responsible, motivated and efficient each morning. I hoped that, if it had that effect on him, it would be the same for the boys.

I did lots of other exercises with the boys to help them to express themselves better. We did a series of paintings using whatever colours, types of paint, brush strokes and textures we felt were appropriate to reflect different moods. The boys and I also did self-portraits (using a mirror) and portraits of each other using different facial expressions and then discussed them. If you are not good at art, these can be simple line drawings. I played lots of different types of music and they painted to the rhythm, tempo and timbre of the piece and discussed how the different types of music made us feel. Please note that you don't have to be a budding artist to enjoy and benefit from doing this. You are not trying to paint a masterpiece. It is more about using the colours, brush strokes and textures to reflect your emotions and provide a place for discussion, so there is no right or wrong, or good and bad art. When Luke did his 'anger' painting he soon complained that he had made a 'right mess of it', which was no surprise to me, as he ferociously swirled all the colours round, adding more and more reds and blacks. Then comparing his to my 'anger' painting he found that incredibly mine did show anger, but that it was 'controlled anger', and although the sharp red lines looked angry, I had still managed to keep all the colours clean, which he interpreted as meaning that although I got angry, I always remained in control and did the right thing.

As a prelude to other sessions we copied some of the ideas learned from Luke's therapist (she is a music therapist). We used the few musical instruments that we already had and also made more by filling different jars and bottles with dry foods such as pasta, lentils, rice, etc. Some we used as drums, together with pots and pans, and others we used as shakers. We found other objects that we could rub a stick against to make different sounds. We then played games where one person had to set the beat and the others joined in, then changed the order. We picked different instruments for each other, or picked different instruments to represent different feelings. When we first started doing this we seemed to make an awful noise, but after several attempts we all seemed to get the hang of it and actually managed to sound in harmony. As with the art, this exercise is not about making beautiful music, but about creating rhythms and noises to express how you feel, and it is a great warm-up exercise if you want to lead into a more in-depth discussion or exercise.

Safe o'meter

This started with an exercise that Luke's therapist did with him. 'Yellow dot' people are safe and 'red dot' people are extremely dangerous (like bullies, criminals and murderers) 'orange dot' people appear safe some of the time, but you always have to be on your guard and can't trust them, as they have many of the characteristics of 'red dot' people and you never know when they will change. His therapist asked him which dot represented his birth mum. The answer was 'Red, definitely red!' She then asked about his birth dad, 'Orange dot, because he at least tried some of the time'. She then asked about us, 'They are yellow dot, very yellow dot. They are the most "yellow dot" people I know!' he replied. (Phew!)

The idea of the safe o'meter chart is for each boy to identify just how safe he is being at any given time and for him to start being able to identify how safe other people are being so that he can begin seeking out the 'yellow dots' to associate with and have as friends. To reinforce this we asked Luke to make a list of all the 'yellow dots' he could think of. This list included:

- us
- our family
- our friends

- some of his friends
- neighbours
- teachers
- the clergy
- medics
- the police
- judges
- social workers.

We used the safe o'meter in three ways with the boys to ask and emphasize issues around safety:

- By asking 'How safe are you going to be today?' we planted the idea of being 'safe' in their minds and prepared them for the day ahead.
- To highlight how safe other people are being, we helped them get used to finding the 'right' people to mix with and trust.
- By asking 'When you did that, how safe/unsafe were you being?' we introduced a way of helping them identify their unacceptable behaviours and start taking responsibility for their actions.

Effort o'meter

I devised this gauge based on the boys' karate lessons, the idea being that the more effort they put in the better the result. In karate they need to focus and concentrate, because if they don't, they may well get hurt. Their teacher encourages them to give 110 per cent effort to everything they do (yes, I know there is no such thing as 110 per cent, but you could say that '110 per cent' is a distinction in itself), which is not only helping with their karate, but their concentration at school and everywhere else in life is improving. We used the effort o'meter as a way of focusing each morning by stating how much effort we are going to put into our day and refer back to it if they start to slip by asking, 'How much effort did you put into that?'

Esteem o'meter

This is about how they feel about themselves at any given time:

- How do you want to feel today?
- How positive is your attitude today?
- How did you actually feel about yourself when you did that?
- And what was your attitude then?
- How do you want to feel for the rest of the day?
- Is there anything you need to do now so that you can draw a line under that (maybe apologize) so that you can move on and feel great for the rest of the day?

They also get to see that their behaviour *does not* affect the way Chris and I feel about ourselves, which is important as they start to learn that there is no point in playing games or trying to trick us if they have no effect.

Progress chart

As the boys progressed and got older we devised ever more sophisticated charts to monitor their behaviour. As they loved receiving their pocket money each week we decided to use this as a motivation tool in that, if they behaved well, they could receive more money. With this in mind we made the Progress Chart. We used the same one for both of them, using a different coloured line to differentiate between them. Each day we asked them to score how well they had coped on a 0 to 10 basis, with 0 representing awful behaviour and 10 being exceptional behaviour. At first they were confronted by this as it meant that they had to think for themselves and make choices; however, with a bit of encouragement and a few threats of a zero score, they soon started participating fully.

The benefits of allowing them to choose their own score were enormous. It gave them the chance to 'own' and be responsible for their behaviour, showing them that it was really up to them to decide how they wanted to choose to behave. It also gave them the opportunity to reflect on the way they behaved each day, and really notice and take on board which of their behaviours had and hadn't worked, and where they got stuck. Through discussion with Chris and me they were then able to

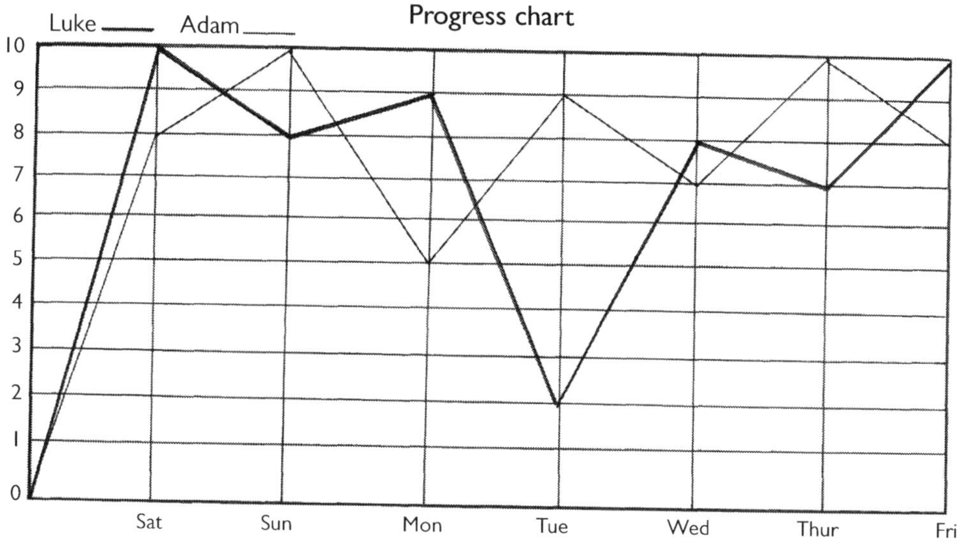

Weeks	Target points	Luke's points	Adam's points	Bonus points	Luke's money	Adam's money
1	40	54	57	50	£2.18	£2.14
2	50					
3	60					

The boys took great delight in working out their pocket money each week and noticing the improvement in their behaviour.
By staggering the bonus it gave them the chance to get back in the 'game', even when they had been naughty

Each point equals 2 pence

Figure 8.2: Progress chart

develop better coping strategies for the next time they were faced with the same or similar circumstances.

By staggering the bonus given, it allowed them the opportunity to change their behaviour and get back in the 'game' . This had the benefit of showing them that it is all right to make mistakes, provided they can learn from these, as this is how children usually learn, and also that they can change the way they behave in a moment; all they need to do is make the decision to change.

Chapter 9

Different Types of Behaviour

On many of the courses I attended I was supplied with long lists of the types of behaviours that can be expected from traumatized children. Every child is different and may display any combination and intensity of these traits. It is unlikely that any child will display all of them, especially at the same time. We found that Luke came with many of the behaviours on the list but would often change tactics as he realized that his behaviours were no longer having the desired effect on us. Here are four lists of behavioural difficulties, some drawn from courses I attended with a few more added that I have learnt on the way.

Social difficulties

- Superficially charming with strangers, grandiosity: it was interesting to learn that Luke did a lot of this because he needed to make himself known to adults wherever he went in order to feel that they would look out for him and keep him safe.
- Poor eye contact: this was true for both children, which is why putting charts and posters on the wall had such good effect. I used to find that our best conversations were when I was driving and they didn't have to look me in the eye, or when we were all focusing our attention on painting, cooking or gardening.

- Poor relationships with peers: we needed to do a lot of work on this.
- Fights for control over everything: this was Luke to a tee and Adam followed suit as he got older. We have witnessed many 'interesting' arguments between the two of them and experienced many attempts of them trying to control us.
- Unable to give and receive affection: although Luke did show affection, often his hugs felt very cold and standoffish.
- Bossiness: in Luke's case he was used to being the 'parent' and constantly tried to parent both Adam and me, often telling us what he thought we should do.
- Passively–aggressively provoking anger in others: this was one of Adam's tricks to get Luke into trouble and paint himself as the 'good guy' in our eyes.
- Needing to know other people's business at both school and at home: just after Adam had started his play therapy, Chris and I sat in the kitchen with the door closed and had what was supposed to be a private conversation with Adam's therapist in which we mentioned the 'inner child'. Several days later Luke mentioned the 'inner child' in one of his conversations. Asking where he had heard this, he had no choice but to own up for eavesdropping, as the subject was not the kind of thing that he would have picked up anywhere else. We then learned that his nosiness actually stemmed from his need to feel safe. Since then we have been a lot more open with him.

Emotional difficulties

- Inappropriately demanding or clingy: both boys displayed this at different times, but this trait was particularly prevalent in Adam.
- Lack of affection towards carers, especially mothers.
- Resentment: this was especially so, in that they resented each other's successes, which manifested itself in jealousy.

- Low self-esteem: this is absolutely true for both boys.
- Deep feelings of guilt, 'It was all my fault': this is absolutely true for both boys to the extent that they both had a 'guilty secret'.

Behavioural difficulties

- High levels of anger and even violence towards carers, especially the mothers: Luke lashed out at me many times in the early days.
- Extreme control problems which often manifest in covert or 'sneaky' ways: both boys were particularly good at sneakiness and trickery and took great delight in playing games and tripping us up.
- Oppositional behaviours.
- Constant blaming of others, as they are unable to accept responsibility for their actions: definitely true, we have had to do a lot of work on this.
- Poor impulse control: there have been lots of breakages and spillages in our house!
- Restlessness, constant need for stimulation: Luke needs to be doing something all the time and although this has lessened now, he used to find it extremely difficult to relax and constantly stated that he was bored, even when he had only just stopped doing something.
- Antisocial behaviours.
- Crazy lying: especially about the great times and good things the boys had in the past.
- Early sexual activity.
- Stealing.
- Preoccupation with fire, blood and gore: whilst still in his birth home, Luke was in trouble for starting several fires.
- Cruelty to animals.

- Disrespect of property, high breakage rate of toys and room trashing.
- Engaging in persistent nonsense questions or incessant chatter: sometimes I think Luke suffers from verbal diarrhoea! This is a trait that Adam has now started to enjoy.

Developmental difficulties

- Lacks cause and effect thinking: this has proved to be very apparent in both boys.
- Abnormal eating patterns, hoards or gorges food.
- Lack of conscience and faith.
- Poor personal hygiene, urinating in inappropriate places.
- Poor balance and clumsiness: Luke has always been prone to this.
- Learning lags and disorders: this is definitely true with our boys – there were huge gaps in the boys' learning. As it was so hard to know exactly what they had missed out on, I overcame this by buying a huge range of school lessons and taught them everything again right from the beginning. We did a couple of hours each day during the holidays and, although they moaned at first, they actually enjoyed doing the work, enjoyed having my attention and I lessened their pain by making it fun. I am pleased to report that after a few holidays of doing this, they did catch up and have continued to do quite well at school ever since.
- Loss of skills: what Luke seemed to know one minute, he had forgotten the next. This also showed in the standard of his handwriting in that one day he would have small, neat handwriting and the next he would be writing like an elephant! Knowing this has helped us enormously to understand where he is 'at' at any given time.
- Selective, or loss of, memory: very true.

- Night tremors and/or sleep walking: Luke has suffered badly from night tremors.

Dealing with difficult behaviour

Your child now needs to learn how you *expect* her to behave: what is and isn't acceptable behaviour, how to express her emotions, how to communicate effectively, how to develop her sense of self and how to form strong relationships. She will need a lot of reassurance that you will be with her every step of the way, that you will teach her and fill in the gaps for her. First, she needs to be reminded that she is NORMAL. Remember, if the same things that happened to her happened to you, you might well be behaving in the same way and, although this response is normal, her behaviour is not normal given her present circumstances. She needs to stop expressing herself through her behaviour and put into practice what you've been teaching her about expressing her feelings. She now needs to know what you expect of her and have it spelt out to her that: '*What happened in the past is not an excuse for bad behaviour now! Those things happened back then; they are not happening now.*'

She needs to know that when she gives her feelings to you, expressing herself through bad behaviour is NOT ACCEPTABLE. She needs to know that you understand how difficult it is going to be for her to learn new ways and that it is going to take a huge amount of effort on her part. At times you might appear as though you are being tough, but actually you are doing this to help her; you are her best friend and that is what best friends do. The trick is to get her to want to make the effort and do it for herself.

I remember touching Luke on the heart and telling him that I knew that deep down inside there was a loving, caring boy screaming to be let out, that I understood that it was hard for him because what he needed to do now was take that 'leap of faith' and trust me. I recognized that his only experience of trusting mothers was not a good one and meant being let down. I then got him to stand in front of me, gently leant his head back, opened his mouth and shouted (quite loudly), 'Hey, you in there. It's time to come out. It's safe here, so you've got nothing to worry about. You've got a mum and dad who love and care for you and they know how to help you. So come on now, it's safe to come out!' This, of course, was followed by lots of giggling. It also had the desired effect.

With your child, tell her that her old behaviours don't serve her any more. Those behaviours were great back then when she needed them. They were her survival mechanism. They worked then and helped her to survive. Congratulate her on surviving. Tell her that she no longer needs to behave like that because she is safe now. It is time to give those old behaviours up and, as in our family, nothing bad will happen to her. Tell her that not only are these old behaviours unacceptable to you, they are unacceptable to everyone else as well and that they are letting her down. Tell her that most people did have a normal upbringing, they did learn the lessons they needed to learn at the right age, and they find her behaviour odd. Other people don't understand that she had gaps in her learning, or suffered trauma and abuse. To them she is a regular looking kid. They don't know that she has painful emotional scars on the inside and, since other children don't understand adoption, to everyone else she is just weird.

To drive this home further, we asked the boys to consider what life was like for Chris given that his face is scarred. You could of course ask your child to imagine someone with a scarred face and what life was like for that person. I pointed out how every single day, people stare at him. Some even make comments, many walk up to him and ask him what happened, some tell him of some accident that they had, others are rude and aggressive, some turn away, because they can't bear to look at those scars, whilst others assume that just because he has scars on his face he is mentally deficient in some way. My point is that because people tend to make judgments and assumptions based on what they can see, it is really hard for them to understand when a child who looks so normal behaves in a peculiar fashion. They can't see their scars because they are internal. Ask your child what she wants other people to think of her: and most importantly let her know that you have confidence in her, that you don't think that she is a hopeless case, that you truly believe she has the strength and ability and is capable of changing her behaviour.

You need to be prepared for the fact that things may well get tougher for you before they improve. It will be scary for your child after years of protecting herself to allow herself to be vulnerable and trusting. It may take many attempts. Your child needs to push and test the boundaries to the full extent in order to understand what they are and ultimately will learn that she can 'get away with' whatever you are prepared to 'put up with'. So it is imperative at this stage that you are firm, and even though you will most probably feel that you are being over strict, hang in there. The results and rewards for both your child and you will eventually pay off and be worth it.

I remember being advised to think about what we were and were not prepared to put up with and only concentrate on the issues that were most important to us, because these damaged children might not amount to much and that we really shouldn't expect too much of them! The trouble with this advice is twofold. If we accepted this as true, the children would have little or no chance of raising their game as if we believed it and responded accordingly then they would too. We also felt that by accepting it we were letting our own standards drop, which didn't feel right as we had worked for years on our own development deciding what our own core beliefs, standards and values were and that now it was being suggested that we drop, or at least lower, them. We felt as though our own integrity was taking a battering and we weren't prepared to let this happen. We consequently decided that we needed to stick to our guns, do whatever it takes to have the children understand that this is what is expected of them in this family and shoot for the stars. If they then only reached the moon, then that would be pretty great.

Anger

You need to let your child know that it is perfectly normal to get angry sometimes. What she now needs to learn are what are and aren't acceptable ways of dealing with this. Ask her what she feels like when she gets angry. If she feels she needs to scream, take her to the top of a hill and let her, or give her a pillow to shout into. If she says she feels as though she is about to explode with energy, give her something physical to do, like running around a field or bouncing on a trampoline. If she wants to lash out and thump someone, give her a punch bag or pillow to hit. With Luke we pointed him in the direction of a large teddy and were delighted to find that he immediately stopped lashing out at us. The novelty of being allowed to bash the teddy soon wore off and so he survived this experience too!

I have recently heard from one particular source that letting go in this way is not necessarily a good thing to encourage as it can lead to violence. The thought is that, if the child is in a situation where she is angry and there is no punch bag or whatever available, then she may resort to hitting a person instead. Having said this, it is deemed acceptable if the whole family is using the same punch bag to vent their anger on as the child will then recognize that it is normal to get angry. I myself can see no harm in hitting an inanimate object as long as the action is supervised and controlled and you have explained that the object is to be hit in place of hitting a person, especially if you also put in place a strategy to use when the child is angry and away from the home/punch bag. We therefore gave Luke a couple of options: he could punch the air or, better still, he could close his eyes and visualize the teddy and then picture himself hitting the teddy in his mind. This is probably the better option as no one would actually know what he was doing.

I have also recently experienced for myself the sheer joy of letting go of my pent-up anger in a most unexpected way. Please note that I am telling you this with my tongue in my cheek. I am definitely not suggesting that you try this one at home. Our family was invited to a 'family fun day' with Chris's company. Luke challenged me to one of the games, and in the general spirit of the day I accepted. The object of the exercise was to balance on two very wobbly podiums whilst bashing each other with foam filled paddles. The first one to knock the other off was the winner. I was determined to win as not only did I want to maintain my dignity in front of Chris's work colleagues, but I was actually afraid of falling and hurting myself even though there were padded mats to land on.

I managed to bash Luke several times, but no matter how hard I tried, he stood his ground. He then (very stupidly) suggested that I took out all my pent-up anger on him for the way he'd treated me over the years, all the times he had played games, all the times he'd tried to trick me and all the times he'd been horrible to me. The poor lad didn't stand a chance and I knocked him flying. What I found interesting was that I learned for myself that if anger is channelled and used in the right way, it can be extremely powerful and effective. As we then decided to make it the best of three, I got the chance to wipe him out again. I could actually feel the sensations in my body as the anger rose within me as I thought to myself, 'This one is for the time you… And this one is for the time you…' The overall effect as I again sent him flying was exhilarating and incredibly freeing. So next time you hear me say that I never bash my kids you will know that I am lying!

From this experience I can see that an exercise some therapists use would be really beneficial. I have seen this done with punch bags (in a gym) representing the people that have hurt your child, life size cardboard cut-outs and stacked up cardboard boxes with people's names and the emotions they induced written on them. If you choose to use this method, the idea is to have your child fully imagine and connect with the person/people with the punch bag/cardboard cut-out or pile of boxes and remember a particular time when something happened. The more your child associates with the feelings that she experienced at that time and the person/people involved, the more powerful the release will be. Then let her say or shout whatever she wants to get it off her chest. You can then let her punch/kick or knock the boxes/cardboard cut-out/punch bag to release all the feelings that those people caused her to feel. Or she may choose not to retaliate at all. This might happen if you point out that perhaps, as an older child, she may be able to see and learn something from that situation that she couldn't see before (as she was so young) and she may actually be able to forgive them.

Dealing with aggression aimed at you

Our boys took up karate as a way of letting go of their aggression and have learned how to channel their energy and defend themselves. When Luke first came to us he was often aggressive, and shouted and complained loudly when we had to restrain him (to protect both him and us). So we pointed out to him that we would stop restraining him if he in turn stopped kicking and lashing out at us: 'If you want me to stop holding you, stop hurting me'. If you are your child's punch bag, tell her (when she is calm) that this doesn't work for you and that she is not allowed to do it any more. Tell her that you know that she has been hurt, is feeling bad and that you understand that she is having trouble communicating those feelings right now. Remember she is giving you her feelings because you are supposed to know what to do with them. This, of course, goes hand in hand with finding another outlet for that anger as just mentioned and teaching her about learning and voicing her emotions.

In return (again best explained when you are both calm) she has to understand that she is now repeating the pattern. You can remind her of the exercises done earlier when we were talking about her family history and breaking the pattern. By hurting you the abused has become the abuser. Ask her if that is how she is going to treat her own children or whether she wants to break the pattern. If she gets stuck, help her. Tell her how you feel when you get angry and suggest other ways she might or could be feeling. A good phrase to use here might be, 'If I had experienced the same things as you and was feeling as angry as you are I might say...and do...' She needs to be aware of the pattern and then agree to break it. Thank her for trusting you enough to know what to do with her angry feelings. Then remind her that it is not acceptable for her to do this any more and that together you will find a new way of dealing with her aggression.

In my own experience I find I am able to get rid of most of my negative emotions simply by verbalizing what they are. 'I am feeling very angry about this...', or, 'Now your behaviour is beginning to agitate me...', 'I feel very sad that this has happened...' So with the boys, I always acknowledge how they are feeling by saying, 'I am guessing that you are feeling pretty angry right now... Am I right?', or 'I understand that you are angry right now', or 'If I were you, I'd probably be feeling quite angry about...' Be careful not to follow these statements with a 'but' because a badly placed 'but' will negate what you have just said and deny your child those feelings. The trick is to get her to admit to and acknowledge her angry emotions. Then, when she has done that, you can ask what she needs to do to turn this around so she can start to feel better. This will have a much greater effect than retaliating and getting angry back, as it will start to get her unstuck (from being angry) and move her on to thinking there is a better way to feel. By doing this you are also teaching her that she has the power within her to alter the way she feels at any given time, and if she chooses to feel good, she can.

Note that since writing this I have qualified as a neurolinguistic programmer (NLP) and a time line practitioner. Through this I have learned effective ways of dealing with negative emotions and limiting decisions. This is great as it gets to the root cause of the problem, dealing with the very first time our children ever experienced anger (or other negative emotion), learning what they need to learn from that event and then dealing with every subsequent time they ever had cause to experience anger again (or other negative emotion). This does not mean that they won't ever experience that emotion again, but it will free them up from all their negative emotions from the past. This obviously needs to be done by a fully qualified, registered and insured NLP practitioner, preferably one who is used to dealing with children's issues.

Dumping sessions

The way Chris and I have always dealt with our frustration or anger, especially after a trying day, is to have a 'dumping session'. We have taught this technique to the boys and it has proved incredibly successful as a way of dealing with day-to-day frustrations, as a way of letting go of the anger and pain incurred from the past, hatred towards their birth parents, and as a way of clearing the air between any number of, and any combination of, the family.

The objective of 'dumping' is to make the person dumping (the 'dumpee') feel better, not for the person listening to feel bad. The rules for dumping sessions are:

- Make it clear that you are going to have a dumping session.
- The listener should ask the 'dumpee' how much time she thinks she is going to need to dump. The session should then be timed and strictly adhered to. Five minutes is a good place to start.
- During that time only the 'dumpee' is allowed to speak, unless it is to offer a few words of encouragement about what a good job she is doing of dumping.
- When she has finished, ask her if there is anything else she needs to say. If there is, ask how much more time she is going to need and set the timer again.
- If you are the listener, all you have to do is 'get' how frustrated, angry, or miserable the other person is feeling. You

must not do or say anything other than to encourage the dumping process.

- At the end of the session, ask her if she feels better. Then and only then you can ask if there is anything she wants help with, or if she wants any advice. Don't be surprised if she doesn't want any, because all she needed to do was dump.
- Anything you hear in a dumping session must not be used as evidence against the 'dumpee'.
- No sanctions, punishments or consequences should be given.

For the boys we added the following rules:

- You can only dump between yourselves if one of us is present.
- You must always ask permission for a dumping session (although it is all right for us to remind them of this process by asking them if they need a 'dump').
- During a session you may stomp about as much as you like.
- You may be as loud as you like.
- You may use whatever language you like.
- You must respect me/us physically.
- You must respect each other physically.
- You must respect yourself physically.
- You must respect the furniture.

If your child finds this hard to start off with, give her a demonstration of how she might do it. She may have a good laugh at you, but she will get it, especially if you let her see that this is how you deal with your anger and that it is perfectly normal to want to let off steam. Children need to know that it is both normal and okay to get angry, but it is what they do with that anger that is important. Using this with Luke has proved enormously beneficial. He no longer takes his anger out on us, or our property, physically.

Before we put this technique into practice, we used to go for weeks at a time without Luke telling us if anything 'not so good' had happened at school. He would always avoid those conversations and rant on about what a fantastic day he had had. Then as we got wiser and started using the 'loving step', we started to ask specifically if anything 'not so good' had happened, or if there was anything that he was afraid to tell us about. It wasn't necessary to use this technique for every little thing, but it was great on the days when he really came home in a tizzy. We found that by giving him an approved method to release his anger and frustration it wasn't long before it started to diminish.

Role play

Another way of dissipating rudeness or anger is for me to repeat back to the boys through role play the way they have just behaved. In fact I use role play for all sorts of things, like having a friend round to play, as mentioned earlier, or practising a particular conversation with a friend or teacher that they are anxious about. So, for example, if Luke moans about having to do his homework and goes into 'Why do I have to do this?' mode, I repeat his mannerisms and protestations whilst washing their lunchboxes and preparing their lunch for the next day, or whatever I happen to be doing at the time. Of course I lay it on thick. 'Why do I have to keep doing this day after day? Why me? I'm fed up with it. Every flipping day it's the same old thing and it's not just that I have to make the wretched lunches; you both like different things and I have to come up with ideas all the time. Then I have to go to the shops, buy it and lug it all home. I wouldn't mind but it's not *my* lunch. I'm not going to get to eat it. I usually just make do with some crackers and fruit. It's just not fair.' I usually include a bit of foot stomping for good measure and throw a bit of a paddy. Get the picture? It usually results in rolling around laughing, but he does get the message and gets to see how ridiculous he has been.

Another technique is simply to reflect their face and actions as though you are their mirror, so that they get to see how ridiculous they have just been. Luke has recently said that he finds this particularly useful and fun and has affectionately named it 'Self-cology'!

The vicious circle of behaviour

One day when I'd had enough of their constant bickering, I sat them down and told them that I was going to introduce them to a new distinction. I told them that every time they argued they were creating a 'vicious circle of behaviour'. I set about explaining the concept by drawing the following:

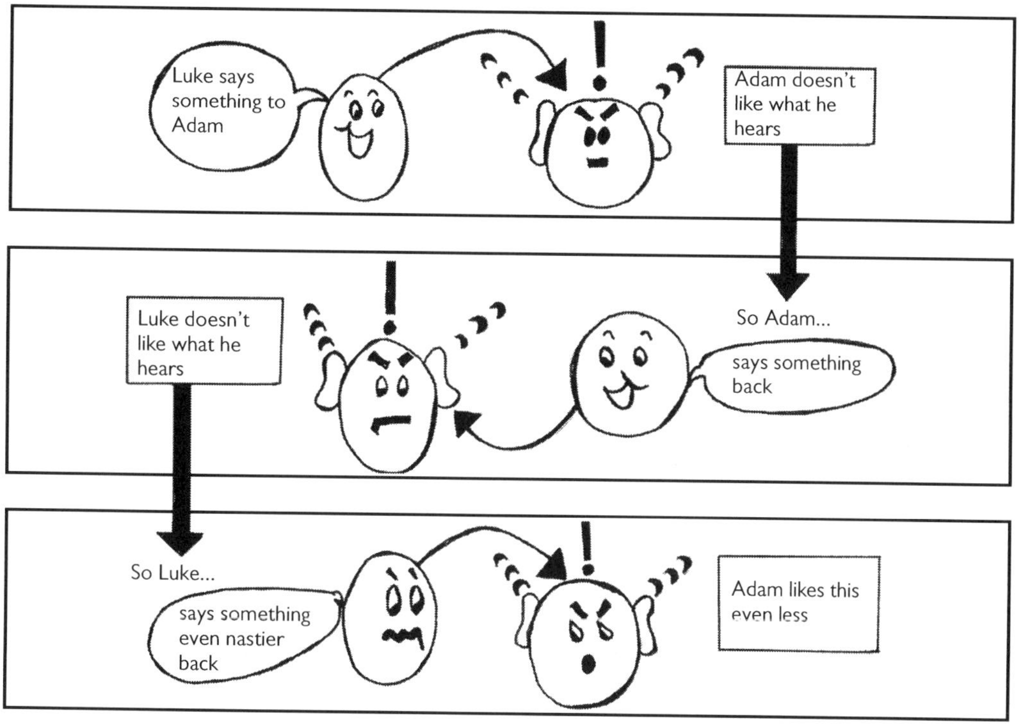

Figure 9.1: The vicious circle of behaviour

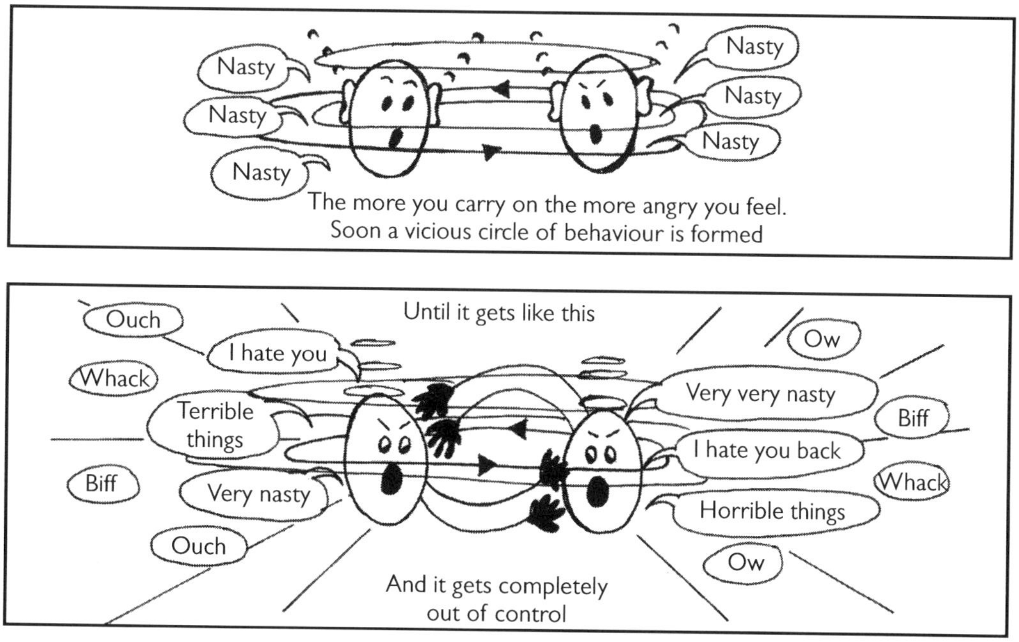

Figure 9.2: The vicious circle of behaviour runs out of control

- One of you will say something nasty.
- The other then answers back, getting even nastier, which winds the other up.
- So he gets even nastier.
- He in turn gets even nastier still.
- And so it goes on until an absolute mess has been created.
- By which time you are both so wound up and so hurt and angry that you start to hate each other and then you start to lash out.
- Then one of us has to intervene, but you don't like that because you hate being told off and like it even less if we shout at you.
- Then as a consequence you lose the opportunity to do whatever it is that you really wanted to do.

I could tell by their faces that I had them now, so asked them what the solution was. They answered that they needed to be different, but of course had no idea of how that might work or how they would be able to stop themselves. I told them that they were right and that what they needed was a 'strategy' for handling it differently next time. They suggested that they came and told me every time that one of them said something nasty. I pointed out that wasn't really a solution, as they would constantly be relying on me to sort out every little argument, whereas the only real solution would be for them to stand on their own two feet, and take responsibility for the situation and their behaviour by recognizing that the inevitable would happen if they retaliated.

The only way to break the 'vicious circle' was to be different by recognizing for themselves what they were doing and to 'BREAK THE PATTERN'. If one of them said something nasty the other could draw his attention to what he was doing by saying, 'That was a bit nasty wasn't it?', or 'That was a bit mean. I'm sure you don't really want to be mean', or better still, 'When you say things like that, it makes me want to start a vicious circle of behaviour!'. Amazingly this simple exercise has had an enormous effect, especially as each time they slipped up and forgot we reminded them by saying, 'Right now you are creating a vicious circle of behaviour. Is that what you really want to do? What do you need to do right now to have it be different?' By repeatedly drawing their attention to this each time they fight, it allows them to internalize it and sink into their neurology until it becomes second nature.

Figure 9.3: The only way out is to break the pattern

Soon they will start recognizing for themselves when things are about to escalate and actually prevent it from happening. What's great about this is that these distinctions give you a way of handling confrontation that is so different from anything that they will have heard before. Also, wording it this way sounds funny and we've found in our house that it is very difficult to stay angry when something makes us laugh; therefore, using this technique never fails to have the desired effect. It also saves us (as parents) from all the angst and stress of having to break up yet another fight or argument and gives us a different way of handling these situations so that our energy and patience remain intact. The only answer they can ever give when you point this out to them is, 'Break the pattern'.

This analogy can also be used to show them the repeated patterns that their birth parents (possibly) inherited from their parents (as seen earlier in the book). In fact it is a very good idea to point this out to them. If they agree that they don't want to make the same mistakes as their birth parents, then 'breaking the pattern' of the vicious circle in this context will have an even greater effect.

Swearing

When Luke came to us he had a full repertoire of foul language. To the boys' surprise we told them that they could only use a swear word if they knew the meaning, and that once they did know the meaning, they then had to decide for themselves if it was still a good idea to say that word. We also said that if they didn't know what a word meant they could come and ask us at any time, providing we were out of earshot of others. If we knew the meaning we would then tell them. What we found was that, rather than tell them they couldn't use a word, it was more effective for us to ask them how they thought other people would think of them if they were heard using this word and then letting them decide. We also pointed out that anyone might overhear what they were saying if they were outside. We live in a small town and the boys have had a lot of contact and interaction with older people, having visited several old people's homes and the British Legion with their school. When I asked them how an older person might feel if they heard them arguing or swearing with their friends, they recognized immediately that they might frighten them and they definitely didn't want that.

Allowing them this freedom, and allowing them to use whatever language they liked in dumping sessions, somehow stopped them from wanting to swear at other times, maybe because they saw that we were putting our trust in them by giving them the responsibility, or maybe it is because it's just not fun if you are allowed to. In a similar vein, I have also heard that some people allow their children a set time when they are allowed to swear or use whatever language they like. So, for example, Friday night might be 'swear night', or if you really can't stand it for that long, allow them to have an hour.

Chapter 10

Control Issues

It is important to realize that all the battles you have with your child will be about power and control. This all stems from their need to feel safe and the early survival strategies that they devised as and when they were needed. If they don't have control over us and our actions, or in fact any given situation, then they are in a 'state of fear'. It is this state of fear that produces their controlling behaviour. It is not about them *wanting* to have control over you, even though it will probably feel (to you) as though they do. Luke became the 'man of the house' when his father left the family home before Luke was three, just after Adam was born. Not long after this Linda, suffering from postnatal depression, started to 'go off the rails', got in with the wrong crowd socially, and things started to go horribly wrong. Luke therefore not only got used to parenting and providing for both Adam and his half-sister, when she was born, but he constantly told Linda what to do, as she was often incapable of thinking for herself and she came to lean on him as her emotional crutch. Having had that much power at such an early age, it is then very hard to give it up.

Luke was excellent at creating situations where, no matter what we did, he won and we lost. He had a knack of setting us up so that whatever we did, we were the bad guys, we were wrong and he was right. An example of this was when I bought him a new pair of shoes for school, which he tried on and had fitted in the shop. Within two weeks he declared that his feet had grown, the shoes were too small, and we should buy him some new ones. Feeling his toes in his shoes, it felt as though he had plenty of room, but he persisted to moan about them and us, leaving us feeling that he was questioning our integrity as parents and in a dilemma as to what to do. It really felt as though he was playing games with me, and as money was tight at that particular time, I was being careful with every penny I spent. I was very tempted to ignore him, but my common sense prevailed, in that perhaps what he meant to say was that the shoes were uncomfortable and I really didn't want to cause damage to his feet. Subsequently I bought him yet another pair of shoes, but I swear there was a glint in his eye!

He had a knack of twisting the meaning of everything we said and did (which is like selective hearing) in order to justify his conditioned belief, which was that he could trust no one, especially adults, as adults let you down. If we asked him to do something he would then delegate it to Adam. Adam looked to him constantly for guidance and let Luke's behaviour set the tone. We constantly had to tell Luke, 'You are not his parent', and that he had no right to tell Adam what to do. More infuriating (for me at least) was the fact that he thought it was his job to tell me what to do. Of course, I soon knocked that on the head, as I wasn't having any child telling me what I should and shouldn't do. So in sheer desperation one day, I waited until he was calm and then had the following conversation:

ME: What feelings do you want to get when you try to trick and control me?

LUKE: I want to be the boss.

ME: Okay. What feelings does wanting to be the boss give you?

LUKE: I don't know.

ME: Is it because you want to be caring and kind? What do you want to get from it?

LUKE: I want to be in control and safe.

ME: Anything else?

LUKE: Yes. I want freedom and I want to be responsible.

ME: Good. So when you try and trick and control me, what you really want is to be in control, be safe, have freedom and be responsible?

LUKE: Yes.

ME: Okay. What actually happens when you try and trick and control me?

LUKE: You get angry and I get into trouble.

ME: Then what happens?

LUKE: I get a consequence or have to sit on the stairs.

ME: That's right. Does that make you feel in control and safe? Do I then give you more responsibility and freedom?

LUKE: No. I just get the consequence and then I get to feel stupid.

ME: So can you see that the things you want to get from controlling behaviour are the very last things that I am going to give you?

Luke had a revelation!

ME: So, if you want to be in control and safe, if you want more responsibility and freedom, what do you need to do?

LUKE: Give up trying to control you.

ME: That's right. All those games and tricks you have played on Dad and me – trying to trick and control us – you can simply give up now. They don't work and they certainly don't give you what you want. You don't need to do that any more.

I then backed this up by asking him to write down all the things he had missed out on recently as a result of him trying to trick and control me and me giving him consequences. The list included:

- I didn't get to play at my friend's house.
- He wasn't allowed round here.
- I wasn't allowed to watch television.
- I didn't get to play on the PlayStation.
- I had to go to bed early.
- I got to sit on the stairs.
- You didn't take me to the park.

This really happened and my approach with him really worked. He did stop playing all those horrible hurtful games. So I quickly rewarded him by giving him some more responsible things to do, which was great because he kept thanking me for trusting him enough to be responsible.

Consequences

You will have noticed by now that some of your child's behaviour is purely attention-seeking and is best dealt with by ignoring it. For example, Adam's whining was dealt with by us saying, 'There's no need for that', or 'Adam, you are whining. It is not necessary to whine'. Once he was aware that this is what he was doing and that he really wasn't getting the extra attention that he wanted, he soon stopped. Likewise we said the same when Luke used to hit himself on the forehead. Similarly Luke soon gave up his tantrums as we simply used to walk out of the room without even a comment. He quickly learned that there is no point in having a tantrum without an audience.

Chris and I have also developed our own language. Rather than scream at them every time I catch them starting to do something wrong, I often make a deep and very purposeful noise that sounds like 'hut' with a lot of emphasis on the 't'. I may also say, 'I don't think so', with an air of authority as I wag a finger, and I have developed a raised eyebrow look, that lets them know when I disapprove. Another favourite is a loud and meaningful 'Oy!'

Choices and outcomes

As a way of getting the boys to take responsibility for their behaviour, we started to teach them that:

THERE IS NO SUCH THING AS BAD BEHAVIOUR. THERE ARE ONLY DIFFERENT CHOICES AND DIFFERENT OUTCOMES.

In other words, *they always have a choice as to how they behave. It is up to them to decide what kind of day* they *are going to have.*

We felt it was important for them to see that it was time for them to accept that they were responsible for their behaviour and that it was us not them who set the atmosphere and tone in our home and that we were going to carry on with our lives regardless of how they decided to behave at any given time. If they couldn't handle it, because they couldn't behave, they simply couldn't join in with whatever we had decided to do. This was tough, especially on birthdays, Christmas, etc. At first we felt guilty because we really wanted them to be there participating. However, it didn't take many missed events before they started to realize that we meant what we were saying. 'Thank you for showing me that you are not able to handle your behaviour and join in right now...'

If they decided to behave well they got to join in and they found that pleasant outcomes or consequences occurred naturally. If they chose not to behave well, there would not be such pleasant outcomes or consequences. In doing this we were then able to congratulate them on making their decisions, not necessarily for choosing well, but for making the choice that they had made. We also made comments and asked questions like:

- 'Is that really the way you want to behave right now?'
- 'When you did (that) I thought (this). Is that how you really want me to think?'
- 'It's okay to make mistakes. It's not okay not to learn from them.'
- 'I still love you, even if you are finding it difficult to behave nicely today.'
- 'It's not you I hate. It's the way you are behaving.'
- 'Thank you for showing me that you are unable to handle playing together nicely right now. Maybe next time you play together you will handle it differently.' It is important to indicate that there will be a 'next time' as children often think that once something is said, it is written in stone and that they have blown it forever.
- 'Tell you what, you decide – whether you are going to mess about or not when you get ready for bed... You decide... It is your choice.'
- 'Okay, that's not the choice that I would have made, but well done for making your choice. Now you need to...'
- And if they had had a bad day, we always said, 'Tomorrow is another day', as we tucked them into bed. Adam said this was great as he always knew that he then had another chance.

Some consequences happen naturally:

- 'If you refuse to wear your coat, you might be cold or get wet later.'
- 'If you touch the cooker while it's hot, you will get burnt.'
- 'If you don't wash your hands properly after going to the toilet, you might get worms!'

I often found that I was able to get the response I wanted by simply repeating the instruction using the same tone of voice, as many times as was necessary, thus avoiding confrontation altogether. 'Put your coat on Luke…' 'Put your coat on Luke.'

Another trick I sometimes used in the early days was to say the opposite of what I meant… 'I want you to be really naughty at school today, get into lots of trouble and have to go and see the headmaster…' It is sad that Luke's head used to be so mixed up that this actually worked. Perhaps he could see the ridiculousness in what I was saying, or by then being well behaved it fed his need to defy me and make me wrong.

At first I used to remind them constantly about what the consequences might be for their actions, but I was able to toughen up when I realized that the more I mollycoddled them, the less they were actually learning for themselves and therefore the less responsibility they took for their behaviour. These days I usually just say, 'Okay it's your choice', in a nonchalant way. 'You work out for yourself what the consequences of your actions might be.' I have set up enough routines and schedules for them to know what to do at any time; it's now up to them to remember, for example, to take the right books, etc. to school (though of course I gave them extra help when they needed it, when changing schools, etc.) and accept whatever consequence the teacher gives them if they don't. Having said that, please note that when they first moved in I felt it was important to rush up to school with their lunch, for example if they had forgotten it, as a way of reminding them that they were in our family now and that being in our family meant that I cared for them and that I was prepared to do whatever it takes to show them that I love them.

Now they have learned that and are older, although it might still be tempting to run around after them, I feel it is better that I teach them to be responsible for their actions and learn from each experience. Remember my aim has always been to teach them how to be independent so that they can cope much later when they are adults and out on their own in the world.

Other consequences/outcomes require a bit more thought and for best effect need to be delivered as soon after, and to match as closely as possible, the 'crime'. Having said that, again I have learned the hard way that there is little point in delivering a consequence if I am angry. If I do, it invariably turns out to be over the top, or totally impracticable. These days, for the most part I am much calmer and able to handle whatever behaviours they care to throw at me. Heaven knows I've had enough practice. I have noticed that if they do make me angry and I don't handle my anger well, they have a sense of having won. If they do manage to rattle my cage I now tell them that I am feeling angry and that they need to go to their rooms or sit on the stairs until I have calmed down whilst I think about what consequence I want to give them:

- If they deliberately make a mess, they get to clear it up, or, if for example they have spilt something on the carpet or sofa that I would prefer to clean myself, I give them a different cleaning job.
- If they deliberately break something, I fine them, withhold their pocket money, or get them to do jobs to earn the money to pay for a replacement.
- If they start messing about with their food, it's time to leave the table or better still have them sit there till everyone else has finished. Then there is no more food until the next meal. In this instance I say, 'As you are playing with your food I have to assume that you aren't very hungry right now', as I take their plate away ignoring any protestations (as stated earlier).
- If they are late coming to the table, they either miss that meal completely if they fail to show up before everyone else has finished, or I take their plate away, regardless of how much they have eaten, when everyone else has finished and again there is no more food until the next meal.
- If they can't play nicely and fairly together on the PlayStation, or start arguing over which television programme to watch, I

give them one warning and say, 'If I have to speak to you again about this you will have to turn it off'. If it happens again, I then turn it off saying, 'Thank you for showing me that you can't handle watching television today. Now you must switch it off'. If they argue further, they may lose this privilege for further days.

- When giving loss of privileges I have found it useful to write them on a note and stick it to the fridge or notice board, as it seems to have solved any further arguments about the subject. Writing a note in this way also helps Chris and me know and remember what consequences each of us has given and helps us to follow through on our word. As already mentioned it is also important that you let them know that the consequence is only for a set period of time as children have a habit of thinking that if you stop them from doing something then they have been stopped forever. This in itself can be quite traumatic for them.
- In the early days when Luke used to beat Adam up I used to separate them and then ban Luke from playing with Adam or being in the same room as him unsupervised, for a set amount of time. Often I used to create a bit of pain for him too by getting him to write a letter of apology to Adam. I also introduced the 'no touching rule'. If Luke wants to touch Adam for any reason, even to give him a hug, he has to ask his permission first.
- If they are nasty to me, I occasionally announce that their consequence is that they have to come with me to the shops and help me choose a treat for myself. A fellow participant on a course told me that she did this with her children to great effect. Luke couldn't believe it the first time I tried this when I got him to go with me to the florist's to buy myself some flowers and asked him to help me arrange them in a vase. They served to remind him for days that it wasn't okay to hurt me.
- In the early stages Luke often needed to be controlled whilst walking to school and to the shops. For this we had him hold

one of our hands until he was under control and then let him try again on his own on the proviso that that would be his last chance. This method will work well if you have a pushchair or indeed a shopping trolley as by getting your child to hold on to the handle this is in effect putting them in a 'time out/in'.

- Both boys, but especially Luke, used to play up when we went to the supermarket. As a way of dealing with this I took them with me to do the weekly shop at a well known supermarket that happened to be (at that time) the largest in Europe. For once I didn't tell them how I expected them to behave and just proceeded with the shopping, making sure that I went down every aisle, pausing every now and then, pretending to study labels. When I got to the checkout I found that as a result of them trying to distract me with their normal antics I had missed several items on my list, so I marched them back to the start of the shop and repeated the process. Since then they have been much better. I've also found that if I involve them in the process by asking them to find items, check the prices, read the food labels, then help with putting the things on the conveyor belt and pack the bags, they are usually too busy to play up.

We sometimes play the 'smiling game'. This one is great not just whilst shopping, but for walking down the high street too. The object of the game is to get as many people to smile as possible by smiling at them and then to keep track of the smiles collected by counting them. It is really hard for them to be 'naughty' or rude to anyone at the same time. As they are older now, another useful way of keeping them occupied whilst shopping is to have them try and work out which bargains are real bargains (by doing the maths) and which are just marketing ploys made by the manufacturers. This is great because it not only teaches them how to look after their money, but makes them aware of the power of advertising and the reality of being sucked in by it.

When I first started to give the boys consequences, I used to feel bad and as though I was being too hard. For my own peace of mind I checked this with Luke's therapist and she confirmed that I was just doing what I had to. Since then, as a way of checking, I have sometimes asked myself if

I would give the same consequence to a child who had been born naturally to me. The answer has always been yes. I then reasoned that I was deemed to be responsible, I passed the initial assessment to adopt children and the children were subsequently placed in my trust. The papers all went to court and were read by three judges who also thought that I was suitable to be their adoptive mother. I could therefore in turn deem myself to be trustworthy, make my own judgments, trust my gut instincts and know that I am making the right decisions to improve their wellbeing and stop beating myself up.

Time outs

We have used time outs in several different ways. If the children are playing a game in the garden with us and one of them has got over-excited or silly, we have given them a one-minute time out, or 'time on the bench', which has in most cases proved enough time for them to calm down and rejoin the game. If there are other children present we have used this method with them too without upsetting them or their parents. With our own children we have often found a quiet word in the ear saying something along the lines of, 'Is that how you want to behave right now?' or 'I don't want to show you up and make a fuss in front of your friends. Is that what you want?' usually has the desired effect.

If they have misbehaved in the house, we have often put them on the stairs. Normally this is for something non-specific, e.g. Luke has been rude to one of us, or has tried to twist the meaning of what we have just said. The most effective time to give them is one minute for each year of age. Initially when using this method I used to bend down to their level and in an authoritative voice tell them what they had done wrong and why I was putting them on the stairs, allowing one minute for each year of their age. If they started to protest I would firmly say, 'This is not open for discussion. I've told you what you did wrong. Now you need to sit there', and then walk away. Please note that their time begins only when they are sitting quietly in the allotted place. If they were ready to apologize nicely at the end of their time I would then give them a hug as a way of reintegrating them, showing that despite their silly behaviour I still loved them.

Very occasionally they have not been able to apologize nicely at the end of the set time and so I have repeated the process. It is really important to do this and be firm, otherwise you are telling them that you are not really serious and that you are prepared to let them 'get away with it'. It has never ceased to amaze me that my two sat on the stairs without any further protestations or acts of defiance, right from the very first time of trying this. They did exactly what I said, took their consequence and just sat there. I have since watched many parenting programmes and seen many children who did all kinds of things to get more attention by rebelling against the consequence. If this happens and your child refuses to sit there, you need silently to keep putting them back until they do 'do their time'. In one programme I watched, the mother had to put the child back over 100 times before he finally accepted his consequence. She was extremely exhausted at the end of it but this was greatly alleviated by the sense of satisfaction and achievement she got when he did eventually succumb to her wishes. I have also seen many different variations on this theme, using 'the naughty step, stool, corner', etc. Where you choose is not really important; we just felt that using the stairs provided a neutral territory with few distractions. We have always preferred to call it the 'thinking step'.

As the boys got used to this process I then progressed to the next stage, which was to have them sit on the stairs and ask them to work out what they had just done wrong. After the set time, I then asked them if they had managed to work it out. Usually they had, but very occasionally they needed more time. I asked them to tell me why I put them there before apologizing. If they tell me immediately what they have done wrong, I tell them to sit there and work out how they will do things differently next time. Sometimes I do it slightly differently and tell them to go and sit on the stairs, then to come and see me when they are ready to be sensible again. I always ask them why they think I put them there and what they need to do differently next time. I also ask if there is anything they need to do before they can get on with whatever they were doing again. This might be to clean something up, apologize to someone, etc.

Being stuck

Luke's therapist introduced the concept of being 'stuck'. This is when the child is frozen (Luke's face used to glaze over completely) and is therefore incapable of working it out for herself. Thinking about this made sense as I had heard many times of the 'fight, flight' response that is instinctive to the human race. This is when we are faced with a potentially dangerous situation and are forced to make the decision as to whether we should stand our ground and fight or run away and escape the situation. Less talked about is the 'fight, flight or freeze' concept which I have recognized many times, in that Luke would quite simply freeze in some situations, rather like a rabbit caught in the middle of the road when a car approaches with its headlights on. This was often apparent when he had to make a choice or a decision and his brain was so confused that he just froze. You may need to help your child with this concept a few times before she gets the hang of it. What she needs to say to you is, 'Mum, I'm stuck. Will you help me?' You can help her start to recognize when this occurs by asking her if she is stuck and then asking her what she needs to say to you so that you understand that she is stuck. You can then help her to work out what she has just done wrong by going over the scenario with her and what she might do differently next time, though it is always better to engineer it so that she comes up with the answer. We also came up with a secret word which was 'toffee', to hide Luke's embarrassment at the thought of admitting he was stuck in front of other people.

These children need to learn to work things out for themselves. This method of giving consequences has proved to be incredibly beneficial to Luke, and I will never forget the first time Luke said to me, 'I'm just going to sit on the stairs, Mum; I need to calm down and think'. You could have knocked me over with a feather. We have found that for Adam, this method is not always beneficial, and certainly in the early stages could in fact do more harm than good, as it served to remind him that he was always the one who was left out and so he got to feel isolated, abandoned and unloved – feelings that he chose to have sometimes himself, but only when it suited him (I cover this later). We consequently tend to give him 'time ins', which involve him sitting in the same room as us, and although he is technically still with us, he cannot join in with anything until his time is up and he has thought things through. At the end of a time out/in we always encourage the boys to develop 'coping strategies' so that they can handle the situation better next time.

Micro management

A couple of times when Luke was at his worst and most difficult stage, Chris took over and literally 'micro managed' him. I think the hardest time was the first time Chris ever did it. Luke literally had to stay glued to Chris all day long and as Chris was working in his office for much of that time it must have been terribly boring for him. The concept of 'micro management' proved very beneficial to Luke. Chris started by saying to him, 'As you've shown me that you are unable to take responsibility for keeping yourself safe today, you need to stay with me and I will make all your decisions for you and I will keep you safe'. Everywhere that Chris went Luke had to follow, to the extent that if Chris wanted to go to the toilet Luke had to sit on the floor outside and wait. If Luke wanted to go, he needed to ask and Chris waited outside. It is not the sort of technique that you would want to use too often and I know it would have been very difficult for me to implement. Luke improved greatly after that and, although the experience was repeated a further couple of times, it was never necessary to enforce this method to the same extent as the first time.

Chapter 11

Dealing with the Effects of Difficult Behaviour

Just as a plane is about to take off, the air hostess always goes through the safety routine. As she demonstrates what will happen if the plane loses altitude and the oxygen masks come down, she says, 'You must attend to yourself before your children'. I nearly wrote this chapter first, for that very reason, as it is so important that you take care of your own needs first. If you are a wreck, you are not going to be able to give your children the huge amount of support, help and commitment that they need. I then rationalized that like me you were probably feeling pretty strong when your child first arrived. I also realized that, if unlike me, you work steadily through the processes described in this book you may never reach the depths of despair that I did. If you have reached rock bottom and don't know which way to turn, you have my utmost respect and understanding and I want you to know that I've been there and you are definitely not alone. Oh, and incidentally, if you really are at rock bottom, there is only one direction you can go!

Support

For me, one of the hardest things to come to terms with was that I had little or no support. Although Mum lived with us for nearly two years after the boys arrived, and it was nice to have her around, we did try and keep most of the boys' problems away from her as she was in so much pain with her hip and I didn't feel it was right or fair to add to her discomfort. So apart from one occasion when Chris and I had to go to a meeting, and once when we went out for a drink, I never left the children alone with her and was always in earshot if they went into her rooms.

Please don't get me wrong. I love all my family and friends dearly. They just live all over the country and my brother lives abroad. They live very busy lives and aren't always available to me. I found that often (quite justifiably) they were so caught up with their own families and issues that they had little or no time for mine. I also found it really difficult to communicate effectively the intricacy and severity of Luke's behaviour and the effect it was having on me. When I did confide in other people I was often told that, 'All children do that!', which made me feel that they thought that it was my lack of parenting skills that was at fault, which of course did nothing for my self-esteem (and was probably not what they meant anyway).

At this time Chris was still working in London and the pressures of work were keeping him away from home a lot. At the same time the boys were displaying their worst behaviour ever and I really wasn't coping very well. Just when I needed help most I found it extremely difficult to admit that I was struggling. I felt that the boys and the behaviour they were dishing out had well and truly got to me. The enormity of their issues was beyond what I thought I knew, and although I was desperately searching for solutions by attending courses and reading books, I still wasn't finding the answers I needed.

When I did pluck up courage and ask for help I was told that maybe I just needed to accept that this was how the boys were, and when I tried to explain how damaging I thought it was for the boys to continue seeing their birth parents, I was basically told that I would just have to accept it. This I absolutely refused to do as I couldn't face living the rest of my life like this. I was convinced that somewhere locked deep inside the boys were the people that they deserved and longed to be, but that this was being stifled by their visits into the past.

So at the time when I needed help most I found that all I wanted to do was stay behind closed doors. I convinced myself that to ask for help meant that I was weak, and I was overwhelmed by feelings of, 'I *should* be able to deal with this', knowing everything that I know. Perhaps there was also an element of fear involved, in that to admit to social services that I couldn't cope might mean that they thought I wasn't good enough to adopt these children. Even though on a conscious level I knew this wasn't true, I suspect that my subconscious believed differently.

When Luke was at his worst I sometimes felt that even Chris didn't always recognize just how horrible Luke was being to me, as he was often at work. One woman I met later told me that she had purposely gone away for a week so that her husband got to experience and appreciate the difficulties she had with their child. I started to think I wasn't good enough and perhaps the boys would have been better off with someone else. My self-esteem plummeted. Gone was the confident woman who could stand her ground in the workplace.

As I explain the feelings I had back then, I realize that with all the pressure I was under, it was my confidence that took the battering and bore the brunt of this stress. As a result of this I stopped trusting my gut instincts. I now know that these instincts (had I acted on them at that time) were exactly what we as a family needed. What I needed more than anything back then was a huge boost to my confidence; I needed someone to believe in me and ask what I thought the answers might be and encourage me to put those answers into practice.

It wasn't until our local post-adoption team started a post-adoption support group that I had any real support. I found these meetings invaluable and loved to go and have coffee with the girls, go to meetings each month and finally to mix with people who didn't judge, understood and most importantly had experienced the same or similar levels of despair and frustration. I was pleased to find that, just like me, most of them had no family nearby to back them up, and this helped me realize that I wasn't being weak after all. So if at the moment you are in the 'pits of despair', please understand that this is quite NORMAL and you are definitely not alone.

If you haven't got a support group in your area then ask social services to put you in touch with other adopters, then 'buddy up' or approach other agencies, join Adoption UK, join chat rooms on the Internet, do anything, but please don't do as I did and hide behind closed doors. As I mentioned earlier, there is no school to go to learn how to be parents. When you entered into adoption you took on an enormous and complex job; I have no doubt about your abilities to do a great job. I just know from my own experience how easy it is to become weighed down by the enormity of the task.

There is nothing like adopting a child to bring any unresolved issues you might have of your own to the surface. These damaged children have a way of finding and picking at those sores which we may have been able to get away with, or accept and live with, before the children came on the scene. They need to be dealt with now. You need to be stronger than you have ever been before if you are to get through this and provide them with the level of support they need.

For me, it became difficult to distinguish which were their problems and which were my own, as they became so good at transposing their emotions on to me, and the more time that passed and the better I knew them, the more I became attuned, sensitive and able to pick up on what they were feeling. It wasn't until I was able to recognize this fully that I realized that, by allowing them to do this, they were sapping all my strength. My issues *weren't* the same as theirs and I was actually pretty much sorted out. I was then able to see the way forward, and that meant detaching myself from their problems, freeing myself up to deal with them better. There is no shame in finding a counsellor or a psychotherapist, even if it is just to have someone to talk to about your children and their issues. It is far better to do this than to struggle on alone.

In the adoption assessment process we had to talk about our parents and our upbringing. As a way of putting this into context, it may help if you take this a step further and consider how your parents were brought up too. Really think what it must have been like for them as children. What is their three-year-old child like? And what were their parents like? You can do this even if one, or both, of your parents is no longer with you, and you can certainly have a good guess and use some of the earlier exercises if you were brought up by someone other than your birth parents. What beliefs were handed down to them and then passed on to you in the form of 'conditioned responses'? Decide which beliefs serve you well and keep hold of them. Then decide if any are inappropriate for you, given the way you live your life and what you choose to believe about yourself now as an adult; then let them go. With our children, when I want them to let go of something I get them to close their eyes, then imagine squeezing the thing they want to give up into a balloon. I then have them go outside (in their minds) and let go of the balloon and watch it float up into the sky. Other beliefs may simply need updating. Many of those beliefs you created for yourself as a three-year-old probably don't fit with the way your life is now.

Berating ourselves

A few years ago I read somewhere that how we talk to, or berate, ourselves is probably the way that our parents talked to us as children, which they in turn learned from their parents, which ties in with 'conditioned responses' and how we treat our own 'three-year-old child'.

We are often our own worst critics. Reading this was a revelation to me as I had, for as long as I could remember, woken each morning, berating myself for not being good enough, lacking direction and generally feeling guilty about myself and more recently, guilty that I didn't have all the right answers with the boys. Having had this pointed out to me, I found I was able to give it up instantly and started being much kinder to myself and my 'inner child'. I also read that talking to oneself in this negative way is living by other people's standards and limitations. For those of us who do this, we are much harder on ourselves than anyone else has been. I reasoned that if someone came up to me in the street and spoke to me in such a negative way, I would probably get very angry with them and have rather a lot to say about how rude they were being. It was therefore rather ridiculous for me to be saying those things to myself; after all, I have very high standards and integrity and clearly I am doing the best that I can. I don't deserve to talk to myself like that.

Forgiving our parents

Although in my head I thought I had forgiven my parents many years ago (not that they did anything particularly horrible), I was able to forgive them again on a much deeper level. In fact, these days I'm not sure whether they ever needed any forgiveness at all, as I can see that they were doing the best that they could and could only teach me about things that they knew.

To clarify this further I will share with you what happened to me. Up until the age of eight I loved my mum and dad and life was good. I was happy. I used to leap out of bed each morning full of the joys of spring and race my dad to get dressed. Then one day I remember my parents called me into the lounge because they wanted to talk to me. They told me that Mum was pregnant. I remember touching Mum's tummy and asking if the baby was in there. Had this been all that they had said, I wouldn't have had a problem. Unfortunately it wasn't. They then went on to tell me the story of when I was born. They had arranged to have me at home, which is just as well as that meant that there was already a midwife on standby. Mum was extremely ill, lost a lot of blood and a special team had to come and give her a blood transfusion. As the story unfolded, my father got more and more dramatic, to the point where he blurted out that, as the doctors and nurses kept fussing over me, he had screamed at them, 'Forget about the baby, save my wife'.

Up until then I had been blissfully happy, but those seven words had such an impact on me that my world was turned upside down. Everything I thought I knew went out the window as I made them mean all sorts of things, including: I wasn't loved after all, I wasn't wanted, and I wasn't good enough. Hearing this was such a shock for me that from that moment onwards my 'core belief' about myself and my world was completely changed, 'selective hearing' kicked in, and from that moment onwards I only heard things that reinforced that I wasn't good enough and that I wasn't wanted. I was no longer able to hear any of the many positive things that were said to me. Consequently, I started to mistrust Mum and Dad. I had a horrible time during puberty, gave my parents a pretty tough time through my teens, and I grew up with a huge inferiority complex. I thought I wasn't as good as my brother and sisters and I was also incredibly conscious of my looks. It is of no surprise that I later put on weight to 'protect' myself.

It wasn't until I was an adult that I was even able to remember that the conversation about my birth was the start of all my problems. This was when I started forgiving them, but not before I was able to understand that what my dad had said was exactly what anyone would have said in those circumstances, especially as he could see that I was all right. 'Forget about the baby' didn't actually mean forget me for ever or any of the things I subsequently made up, and I realized that my 'selective hearing' hadn't allowed me to hear all the positive things that they had said to me since that day. Dad's only mistake was saying these words to an eight-year-old, or a more positive way of saying this perhaps might be that he trusted that I was mature enough to understand his meaning. Mum's only mistake had been being there when he said it and not realizing the effect of those words. Truly understanding the process and effects of 'selective hearing' has now left me with the realization that there was never anything to forgive.

I was absolutely amazed, when I had a conversation about this with my mum as an adult, to find that she didn't even remember telling me that she was pregnant, let alone telling me the story of my birth. Yet this single event had been of such importance to me that it had literally shaped my life from then on, to the extent of being overprotective to my sister when she was born, and perhaps that may even have been the reason why I failed to conceive, in that my subconscious mind stopped me from putting myself in the same position. When Mum told me her version of the story of my birth, I was again amazed to find that her recollection was incredibly different to the story I had originally heard and believed to be true.

My point in telling you all this is that I want you to understand just how differently we as human beings interpret information, and that one person's concept of what happens at any given time will be completely different from another's experience of exactly the same event. Having had this conversation with my mum as an adult, I realized just how ridiculous it was that my life had been based on a 'load of twaddle', and that from then on I was determined to let go of that belief and any other beliefs that I might hold to be true, but which were based on decisions I had made at such a tender age.

I have shared this with you for two reasons. The first is that I urge you to look at your own life and recognize if you had any shocks. Work out what your 'selective hearing' might have said about them and if possible talk to your parents or the person who raised you about any such event. Second, I want you to be aware so that if you think you might have said anything to your own child that might have had such an effect on them, you can then clear it up. To add to this, I would point out that it is often the most innocent of remarks (as in my dad's case) that can have the most devastating effect. I have a friend who had a similar shock when her parents told her that they wanted to have a boy.

I am very careful with our children in making sure that they understand fully the really important messages that I want to put across to them and also, if I do shout at them unjustifiably, I do apologize to them later and admit that I didn't handle that situation very well, or if I do think they may have misunderstood something, I go back and clear it up. I have found that they are resilient and that they do understand that we might be feeling a bit under the weather, over-tired or stressed. I have always told them that Chris and I are not perfect and that we are human beings too. We don't have all the answers and sometimes make mistakes, but we do always do the best job that we can at any given time and under any set of circumstances. Having said that, I know it is impossible to live your life scared of saying the wrong thing to your child. So I have explained this process to my children in the hope that they will understand that if they have ever heard anything in the past or hear anything in the future that is particularly hurtful or that shocks their belief system, then they can challenge me. Better that approach, than they spend years with a chip on their shoulder.

Of course, I don't know your own upbringing or the circumstances of your life. The chances are that you had a wonderful childhood and received plenty of love and encouragement. If you are still having difficulty forgiving your parents or the people that raised you, though, it might help if you start by forgiving them for not being the type of parents that you needed, or for not knowing what you needed to learn, or for not being there for you when you needed them. It really is a good idea to let go of any hurt and anger that you have towards them as this can lead to all kinds of resentment and illness in the future.

Forgiving our children

In a similar way I was able to forgive the children for being the way that they are and doing the things that they do, as I was able to reason that they are only behaving in the way that they had learned to behave, given the way their parents treated them and their inherited 'conditioned responses' and 'selective hearing'. I was then able to relate to them as the hurt, vulnerable and totally reliant little three-year-olds inside of them and to understand that emotionally they were only just beginning to learn things that they ought to have learned as babies. I was able to see that they really were doing the best that they could and remembered the following analogy: when a baby is learning to walk, you don't just give him one attempt and then give up. You would never say, 'That's it. You've had your chance – you've fallen over and now you've blown it!', and then never let them try to walk again.

I saw that all the techniques I had been teaching them were a bit like learning to walk. They were, and still are, doing the best that they can and I saw that it would take them many attempts to grasp everything, especially as they had so much to learn. It was my job to keep picking them up, giving them encouragement, reminding them how to do it, showing them how much I loved and believed in them, and then letting them have another go. Putting this reframe on it, I was then able to see that they would one day be able to walk with their new concepts and eventually run with them. I also recognized that even the fastest runners trip occasionally. All I had to do was remember that emotionally I was dealing with toddlers, which helped me to remain really patient with them and keep on doing what I was doing.

Take a holiday from worrying

I was then able to reward myself with a 'holiday' from worrying and feeling guilty about the boys, my concerns about my capability as a parent and desperately racking my brains for solutions to their problems. I decided that a week was probably too long to start off with, so I decided that for the whole of the next day I was going to allow myself to wake up without chastising myself, spend the whole day without worrying, and go to bed and sleep without searching for answers. I told myself that I could worry the next day if I wanted to, but for one whole day I wasn't going to worry. I found that if any negative thoughts did slip out, I was able gently to remind myself that I didn't deserve that, and that for today I was taking a holiday from worrying. It was marvellous! The day soon became a week, then a month. In fact I have never allowed myself to go back to that manic state of desperately trying to find answers to their problems. Interestingly, by allowing myself the luxury of not worrying, this has somehow freed me up, as I often find the answers I need popping into my head.

The next thing to understand is that you too may need to go through a type of grieving process. Maybe your reason for adopting was that you couldn't have children of your own. Perhaps you have experienced failed IVF treatments and you need to allow yourself the space to mourn the child that you didn't have. One friend told me that she felt deprived that she didn't get to buy baby clothes.

For me, it was more about my loss of identity, as I had been made redundant shortly before I entered into the adoption process. In the workplace I had a job title, responsibility and people respected my ability. Since having the boys it felt as though I had lost all interest in myself and what was happening in the world, and unless I was talking about the boys, I had nothing interesting to say. They consumed all my energy and all my thoughts. Taking on the boys shook those feelings even further as in the home I was just a mum, and a disrespected mum at that. It took me quite some time before I was able to turn this around

I needed to mourn my loss of freedom. When the boys moved in it felt as though they were always there needing me and there was no time for me to do anything for myself. This may sound stupid, as one of the reasons I wanted to adopt children in the first place was to fill and complete my life. I guess the reality was very different to what I expected. So just like them, I realized that I needed time to adjust and grieve for my former life before I was able to accept that they had moved in, then reinvent myself and create a new identity for myself.

A long time ago I heard a story about two lumberjacks. They were both extremely good at cutting wood and worked long and hard. The only trouble was that they continually argued about who was the best. One day their boss had had enough of their arguing, so he set them a challenge. The task he set was to see who could cut the most logs by the time he returned. They set about it, working hard, but every now and then one of them walked off and disappeared for a few minutes. The other one thought that surely he must win, but when his boss came back he found that the other lumberjack had cut the most logs. He said that he didn't understand. He had worked hard from the moment his boss left till the moment he came back whilst the other man had kept taking breaks.

The other lumberjack then explained that he hadn't taken any breaks, he had been sharpening his axe!

So, how are you going to sharpen your axe? What do you need to make you more effective? Having recognized the need to grieve for my former life, and the initial shock of having the boys, I was then able to start asking myself, 'What's good about this? What's missing from and how can I improve my own life?' I started by reading through the reports we had written about the boys at various stages for social services, school and the court. I was then able to give myself a massive pat on the back and acknowledge that, although it wasn't easy to see on a daily basis or in the heat of the moment, the boys had made definite and massive improvements since they arrived. I decided that to look after the boys, I needed to be strong. To be strong, I needed to feel happy and fulfilled and so I decided to create times when I could concentrate on me and what I wanted.

Mind maps

I started by asking myself what my needs were and what would make a difference to the way I feel. Given that I am a very visual person, I decided to put all my ideas on paper and started by making a mind map. To do this you need a large piece of paper or a white board. I started by writing my name in the middle and then drew a ring round it. Next I wrote all the key areas of my life that I wanted to work on in a circle around my name, put rings around them and drew straight lines to the first circle with my name in it. The key areas important to me were my relationships with Chris, Luke and Adam, the extended family, friends, health, spirituality and interests. Having categorized the key areas to work on, I then looked at each in turn and was able to break this down even further and kept breaking it down until I got very clear on how I wanted to live my life and had a definite course of action to take.

I have found in my own life that it is remaining stuck with no plan that wears me down. Once I have a plan and start taking action, I start to feel better immediately. I have also found that although sometimes it's great to have something to aim for – a specific target – it is the journey itself that gives the most fun. Breaking it all down like this allows you to take whatever size step you feel like taking at the time, and by working on all areas of your life at the same time it won't be long before you start to see and feel some real improvements. Doing it this way seems to free my mind up, enables me to see things clearly and helps me to prioritize by letting me see and work on the changes that will make the biggest difference. I have often found that when I get going I need to do further maps in order to get to the nitty gritty, so I would do one for each of the categories and then if necessary do another, until I am so specific and so clear as to what I need to do I can't fail to take action. Having made my maps, I then put them on the wall in our office so that I look at them often and keep referring back to them. This way I am able to keep patting myself on the back as I see how I have progressed.

I was really thrilled when the boys came home from school and told me that they had started to use spider drawings, which are exactly the same thing as mind maps. They use them all the time to plan their work. I used them to plan this book, to organize the summer holidays, to plan birthday parties and to help Chris when he was overloaded at work. The possibilities for them are endless.

Realizing that I had a lot more time to myself whilst the children were at school I was able to rekindle my interest in art, history, music, personal development and writing. I started to take more interest in what else is happening in the world. I also know that I function better if I exercise regularly and have found ways to develop my spirituality.

After about two years of having the boys, I realized that I hadn't allowed myself the luxury of having a bath. So I had one, candles, smellies and all! I also took great delight in reading a book for the sake of reading a book, rather than trying to thumb through books aimed at professionals that I found hard going, in an effort to try to find solutions to the boys' problems. I learnt to say no to things too. I decided that if I was going to function well as a mother, I had to recognize that looking after the boys was harder than I had ever imagined it would be. To make myself strong I had to stimulate, pamper and take care of myself. I told myself that this was what I had to do in order for me to be strong enough to look after them.

I decided only to do the things that empowered me and give up things that I no longer enjoyed or hindered me. Likewise, I started to steer away from anyone or thing that drained my self-esteem and energy. I gave up everything that wasn't necessary for us to function well as a family and all the things that seemed like a burden. I also felt it was important to find time for Chris and we started to go out occasionally and have friends round. More importantly I recognized that I am the boys' role model and that they needed to see that it was normal and healthy for me to have a social life and interests of my own. By steering some of my attention away from them I became more balanced and better able to deal with their problems. So after a long time of saying no to things I then found I was able to say yes to the things I truly wanted to do.

Receiving compliments

For a long time after the boys moved in I used to play down their declarations of how good a mother I was as I always thought that they were comparing me to Linda. I would always reply with, 'It's not a competition'. Looking back, it probably wasn't until they said they didn't want to see her any more, and contact was frozen, that I began to appreciate that they really meant what they said and to them I really was, and still am, the best mother in the world. As I recognized that I had been denying their praise, I also realized that I had been denying my own wellbeing, as it is completely natural to think of our own mums as the best mum in the world. So from then onwards I was really going to take their loving comments and compliments on board. Thinking about this further I started to recognize that as a 'typical Brit' I have been conditioned to play down any compliments. So now, even though I often have to make a conscious effort, I receive all compliments graciously and really do accept them. If someone says 'Your boys are really polite', or 'You've done a great job with the boys', I think to myself, 'Yes I have. I really have'. It also helps if I acknowledge the compliment by saying, 'Thanks for saying that', or 'Thanks, I really needed to hear that'.

Another thing that ties in nicely here is that I realized that one of my biggest wishes in life generally was that I had always wanted to make a difference in the world. Thinking about this further, I realized that actually I was already doing this and making a huge difference to two little boys and that I really could be proud of that. I also saw that often in life we go around doing charitable acts. In fact, most people are nice and want to help and contribute to other people less fortunate than themselves in some form or other. Helping others not only helps them, but has a knock-on effect of helping us to feel good. I then thought that a useful reframe might be that the greatest contribution I could give to another person might be for me to let them contribute to and help me sometimes.

One day when the boys had been particularly horrid to me, I decided to reward myself with a long soak in the bath. I asked Mum to supervise them whilst they made a list of all the things that I do for them. When I finally emerged from the bath, I asked them to close their eyes and put themselves in my shoes and imagine what life was like for me and especially to consider how I felt when they were nasty to me. I repeated this exercise often as a way of building their empathy skills, by asking them to imagine how it might feel to be different people from all walks of life, how it might feel to walk in their shoes and how the world might occur to them. I was then able to take this a step further when I did the following exercise on a course I was attending.

Appreciating mum

About four years ago, I was asked to do an exercise on a course where I had to draw a picture depicting my relationship with the boys. I drew the three of us holding hands, dancing round in a circle, whilst I balanced lots of hats on my head. As it was at the forefront of my mind, I left it on the breakfast bar for them to find. I explained what I had been asked to do and why I had drawn what I had. I said that I saw our relationship as being in a kind of dance. The busier we all are and the more difficult their behaviour is, the faster the music plays and the more complicated the steps are. The hats balanced on my head represent all the jobs I have to do as a mother. So, for example, sometimes I have to be a nurse. I then got them to think about and name as many different hats as they could. These are what we came up with: policewoman, judge, cook, manager, cleaner, teacher, artist, gardener, window cleaner, seamstress, secretary, taxi driver, personal shopper and style consultant, ambulance driver, handy man, party organizer, entertainer, painter and decorator. I then pointed out, that on top of all that I was a mother, a wife, a daughter, a sister, a niece, cousin and aunty, a daughter-in-law, a god-daughter and a friend. Phew! I must have got through to them as Luke piped up, 'You know, Mum, maybe we could take some of those hats off you sometimes and help you more'. Ah! I told them that I always appreciate it when they help me and that sometimes the best way was to help me keep my balance by appreciating me, thanking me, behaving well and generally just taking an interest in what I've been up to.

As time has gone on they have got better and better at appreciating me, but just to keep them on their toes, every now and then when they ask me what I've done today, I tell them: 'Today I got up, made my bed, had a shower, got dressed, got you up, gave you breakfast, got you ready for school, took you to school, came home, made the beds, washed up, put some washing on, dusted and hoovered upstairs, washed the kitchen floor, did the shopping, put the washing on the line, had some lunch, rang Granny for a chat, did the ironing, cleaned the bathrooms, picked you up from school, spoke to your teachers, helped you with your homework, cooked the dinner, cleared up, brought the washing in, played with you, gave you a bath, read you a story and kissed you goodnight...so not much really!' We then all fall around laughing.

I have met many adoptive mothers who have said that they feel unappreciated. Putting this into perspective, it is not surprising as this is yet another 'life lesson' that our children have never been taught. Thinking about this I remembered something I learned long ago. 'How can you be treated in the way that you want to be treated if you don't tell people the way you want to be treated?' Ah ha! So I started telling them:

- When you come out from class at the end of the day, I want you to run across the playground and fling your arms around me. I then want you to give me a big kiss, say hello and ask how I am, or how my day has been.
- Sometimes I would like you to notice if I don't feel well and ask me if I am all right, or if I am feeling any better. (I, of course, then thank them for noticing.)
- It would be nice if sometimes you noticed if I was wearing something new, or you could give me the occasional compliment, as ladies like to feel nice.
- Sometimes it would be nice if you noticed for yourself that a job needed doing and did it, without being asked.

- When we go shopping, it would be nice if you offered to help me carry the bags.
- It would be nice sometimes if you asked me if I'd like a cup of tea.
- It would be nice and polite if you held doors open for me.
- I would like it if you noticed when I have done something for you and thanked me.
- It would be nice if you thanked me for a lovely meal sometimes.
- It would be nice if you could come and give me a hug, for no particular reason, etc.

When we are first assessed to be adoptive parents one of the characteristics that social services and other adoption agencies look for is our ability to empathize. It is ironic that what is seen as a positive trait (and is a positive trait) then often turns out to be one of our biggest downfalls, as we suffer from the effects of bad behaviour, transposing of emotions and actually feeling what the child is feeling. Realizing this, and as a way to keep my sanity, I started interacting with the boys differently.

Having acted as a 'life coach' to many different people from very different backgrounds, with all sorts of issues and projects, I introduced this as a way of me distancing myself from the boys' challenges. That doesn't mean that I didn't help them, just that I used this as a way of recognizing that they were *their* challenges, not mine. As their coach I was then free to train them for life, by putting things into context for them, reframing/helping them to see things differently, developing coping strategies for the next time things went wrong, whilst developing their social, communication and relationship skills.

Doing this took away any guilt I had and all those horrible feelings when I had to give them consequences, especially the ones where it meant that they were going to miss out on something (which always made me feel very sad). In hand with this I was able to start relating to them as though they were already the fantastic people that I knew they could be, highlighting all the things that they did well and having them recognize and enjoy the feelings that helping others gave them, and what success and taking pride in themselves brings. From the position of coach

I was also able to view their behaviour differently in that I was able to start asking myself and them more powerful questions. This in turn enabled me to reframe their bad behaviour and see it from a more empowering viewpoint, so that each time they misbehaved I saw it as an 'opportunity for growth' and an 'opportunity for them to learn something' and was able to ask both them and myself more powerful questions like:

- What's good about this?
- What can I/they learn from this?
- How can I/we/you make this better?
- What's missing?
- What do I need to do to improve on this?
- What frame of mind/state do I need to be in to be most effective in this situation?

Of course, we all have good days when everything seems to flow and others when we feel we are not coping well, but for the most part now I am much calmer and far more in control of the boys, their issues, my emotions and my own life. Often I find that I am able to turn their bad behaviour round and we all have a laugh about it. As I have already mentioned, I love imitating their behaviour through role play as not only can I let go of my emotions by expressing them, but it helps them to see that I have a sense of humour and am not afraid to laugh at myself. It is great fun to mimic what they have just done and have a good stomp around the kitchen. Very therapeutic!

Fly on the wall

A great exercise I learned when studying NLP, which I have used several times now when the boys have misbehaved, is to draw three imaginary circles on the floor, one for the child, one for the child to imagine me standing in, and the third for a 'fly on the wall' who will report back in a few moments' time. I then asked them to think through and replay what has just happened and to say how they were feeling when whatever just happened, happened, whilst looking at the imaginary me standing in my circle. I then asked them to step into my circle and take on my persona whilst looking at the imaginary them standing in their circle. I took a moment for them to step into my body and asked them to stand in the way that I stand and really feel as though they were actually inside my body. I asked them to feel what I feel, see what I would see and hear what I would hear. The more they relate to you at this point the better, so I asked them to consider what life is like for me, what my worries and concerns are and think about all the things that I do in the course of my day and what I might hope and wish for, for my family. Then I had them replay what happened, this time viewing and experiencing it through my eyes, and had them tell me about what they have just experienced.

Next I asked them to stand in the third circle/position as the 'fly on the wall' and had them re-run the scene again, this time viewing both of us in the scene as though they were a reporter, asking if they could see anything different from this point of view and also if there was anything that either party could learn from this experience. You may well be amazed (as I was with my children) with the results. Doing this gave them a different perspective and they were clearly able to see what they had just done and the effect that that behaviour had, learn from it and then change their attitude and their behaviour.

Chapter 12

Glimmers of Hope

We started seeing glimmers of hope from quite an early stage. Admittedly they were few and far between to start off with, but they were definitely there. Both boys soon started to understand and show that they wanted to change because they knew that their former life had not been a good one and they didn't want to repeat the patterns and mistakes made by their birth parents. It is helpful to know that a ship spends most of its journey sailing off course before reaching its destination. Likewise, with traumatized children, they spend most of their time off course before they finally attune with their adoptive parents.

The children soon stopped pretending that everything had been wonderful in the 'old days' and started telling it as it was. They often confided in us, relating all the horrible stories about what had happened to them and owning up to all sorts of capers, which their consciences were now telling them were wrong and therefore needed forgiveness. They have repeated the worst stories many times, which I have taken to mean that they are the hardest for them to get off their chests and that they need more reassurance. Each time I have reminded them that I understood that they had had it hard, that I was sad that these things had happened to them, and that they shouldn't have happened. When they confessed to something, I gently reminded them that it wasn't their fault that they weren't supervised and taught better and that they needn't feel guilty or worry about it any more. I then threw in that, if I had been in their shoes, I would probably have done exactly the same under those circumstances, and just to belt and brace it; I asked them if they would do the same thing now, or react in the same way. They always reply that they would never do *that* now.

Having been with us for several months, the children longed to be adopted and frequently asked when this would happen and why it was taking so long. This was made even more difficult for them to accept as they saw a boy we knew as a foster child move in with his 'for ever' family. He was then fast-tracked through the adoption process and was officially adopted in a very short time. We realized that our boys wouldn't and couldn't feel secure until they were adopted themselves, but it was still really difficult for Chris and me, as we had no idea if they would stay with us or how much longer it would take for the outcome to be resolved. We felt as if we were in a permanent state of limbo. We therefore had to reply to their questions as best we could and fob them off with tales of how busy the courts were and they could only fit in adoptions when they weren't dealing with criminals.

It wasn't until they had been with us for just over two years and the adoption finally went through that everything started to fall into place for us all. The children were genuinely thrilled and incredibly proud to be official members of our family. They have often described this as the best day of their lives. At the same time both boys started their therapy and had their life stories read to them, which meant that Chris and I could really get stuck into all the work that we wanted to do with them. Soon into therapy their contact with their birth parents was frozen, which had a huge impact, was a massive relief to us all, and we were all able to relax and fully appreciate what an unpleasant pressure that had been.

Two steps forward, one step back

Next followed longer and longer periods of perfectly acceptable behaviour, where they could 'hold it together' for days at a time. The only problem was that each time we thought we might have 'cracked it', we found that they couldn't keep it up, and we were left feeling bitterly disappointed as they took a step backwards. Once we saw that 'nice' behaviour was possible it was really quite hard not to expect it all the time, and as they eventually reverted to old behaviours it was always a bitter pill to swallow. Despite our earlier protestations about struggling to cope, this was also a difficult time for us as we were often left feeling frustrated. They did progress, however, and the 'good days' turned into weeks then months. As they got stronger and began to digest the concepts we taught them, they gained confidence and started to develop their own sense of right and wrong. The more they decided how they did and did not want to live their lives, the better they got at handling their behaviour.

Many of the lessons we taught them needed to be revisited several times before they finally sunk in and, as you can see in this book, I delivered many of the messages we wanted them to learn in very different ways. Although it was quite hard for us to accept at first, we came to see, and had to remind ourselves, that we, even as adults, don't always 'get' things first time round, so it would be wrong of us to expect them to take on board everything we said immediately. As human beings we can only fully understand and 'get' what we are receptive to at any given time and need to 'get' these lessons again as we get older and our capacity to understand develops. It therefore may take many repetitions of a concept before we can grasp it fully, whereas it takes 21 days to form a new habit and up to ten times of presenting a new food to a child before they like it. Learning a new distinction has instantaneous effect.

Although we were able to start doing some of the exercises and work featured in this book almost as soon as the boys moved in, some of the exercises weren't appropriate to do before we knew the boys were staying with us. So timewise there was a two-year delay in our children's development. There can be no strict guideline in respect of when it is right for you to introduce these concepts to your child. You must trust your own instincts for that. What felt right for us was to introduce all the common-sense stuff as soon as possible and we did this in the first few weeks that they were with us. In doing this we were also introducing them to the idea that this was what was going to happen and what they could expect to happen as the norm in our house. This showed them that there was actually nothing to fear as we always made sure that we ended each session on a high note, with them feeling really good about themselves, so that there was less resistance when we did start tackling the more difficult subjects. They always said that they felt great at the end of a session and as though their sacks (of baggage) were getting lighter and, in Luke's case, that his 'string' was getting straighter.

When we did start looking at the deeper issues we took time to do only what we thought they were ready for, probably introducing a new concept every few weeks to six months, though occasionally we had to introduce stuff out of sheer desperation as a reaction to prolonged bouts of awful behaviour. Although we made sure that they had grasped each concept completely before moving on, we also revised the last concept with them before we started a new one and made sure that we kept these concepts alive for them by putting up posters and introducing them into our everyday language. So I would guess, as a guideline for you, that had we introduced Adam to everything in the time-frame that we would have liked, we would have seen gradual changes and improvements in succession over a period of months.

As Luke had a completely different, far more complex, way of coping with his stress, and it took the intervention of therapy in conjunction with the work that we did, had we again presented our ideas in our desired time-frame it would probably have taken him nine to 18 months before we saw any significant improvement. In fact, there were many small changes over that time which, as I am sure you know, are often hard to detect when you live with your child on a day-to-day basis. Having said that, they needed to be reminded of all the work, both the things devised by Chris and me, and for Luke the stuff he did with his therapist, many times over the following weeks, months and years.

They are still today, nearly seven years later, very much a 'work in progress' and have periods (literally months) of being able to cope, followed by much shorter periods of not doing so well. When they slip, I simply revisit and repeat the appropriate lesson and make sure that that particular concept features a lot in our day-to-day interactions. The bad news is that there is no quick fix; the good news is that as time passes the periods when they don't cope so well get further and further apart. When they do occur they seem to get weaker, are less disruptive, are easier to deal with and last for less and less time, as they can be turned around really quickly. These not-so-good periods now only last between a few minutes and a few days and only last this long as they are so subtle they are sometimes quite difficult to detect. So for Luke it wasn't until he had been with us for nearly four years, and had dealt with a lot of his issues, that we saw signs that he was then able to enjoy the little childhood he had left. We actually found him playing normally, inventing, fantasizing and getting into character. Until then he had behaved like a stressed-out going-on 40-year-old, with the emotional age of two!

Therapy was not an easy process for Luke and took its toll on us all, as we had to travel nearly 150 miles (on a round trip) to see his therapist every couple of weeks. Had we lived on her doorstep she would have seen him far more frequently, and his time in therapy would have been greatly reduced. It soon became obvious that we needed to change the way we went about this as Luke had the journey there to work out how he was going to sabotage the session and avoid doing any actual work as it was so painful for him. We then started travelling there on a Friday evening, had a warm-up session, stayed in a hotel and then had two further sessions on the Saturday, which is when the real work got done. This was more effective, but must have been incredibly boring for Chris and Adam, as they had to hang about and wait for us. I didn't want to take Luke on my own, because occasionally after a session he was upset or angry and I didn't dare take the risk of that whilst driving. Also, Chris and I wanted to show him that we were 'all in this together' and so we continued gritting our teeth. Gradually over the months things did start to improve as the mysteries of Luke's mind were unravelled and the work we did with him on top of that started to sink in.

Triggers to Luke's old behaviours

After a while we came to understand that as Luke reverted to his old ways it was because an antecedent/trigger reminded him of feelings that he had had in the past, although we have still only been able to identify a few of those triggers. So, for example, after a long period of 'nice' behaviour Luke suddenly started getting out of control again. We couldn't think why this might be. Then, after a week or so, I noticed that Linda's photo had been put back on a shelf in his room. I casually mentioned this to Luke and he said that he had been tidying up and found it at the bottom of his toy box. He then made the observation that maybe he had started to misbehave again because he kept seeing her face every day and it was reminding him of the past. This sounded pretty feasible to me, so I suggested that he might want to put the picture into his treasure box, so that he always knew where it was and he could look at it on days when he felt strong. This worked and his behaviour improved immediately.

Another example was that when we had to move house, despite the huge amount of work we did to reassure him, moving to a completely new area meant not only changing schools but changing everything that was familiar to him. Luke completely went to pieces. He displayed the whole spectrum of his old behaviours and tried a few new ones as well. Obviously we were aware of what a huge upheaval it was for him, but it took us several months before we understood that moving away from the town he was born in raised all sorts of issues for him. Part of him was concerned that he now lived further away from Linda and even though we went back to our old town a few times he couldn't comprehend that it really didn't take that long to get there.

In desperation we visited his therapist again (after months of not needing to) and she pointed this out to us. (Actually, with hindsight, this is perhaps one of the more obvious triggers that he has reacted to.) We then remembered to get the map out again and were reminded to have another remembrance ceremony for her. We also thought that making such a huge move might have brought back the feelings of fear he endured when faced with new surroundings and unfamiliar people as he was taken into care. He took several months to get over the move, but eventually he did settle.

Surprisingly to us he handled the move to secondary school very well, possibly because there is a good transition support team in this area and the school was incredibly supportive, with the head of year personally showing him around the school prior to the other children visiting it, indicating to him lots of places to go if he needed to feel safe. Other triggers have proved much harder to detect. In fact, it gave me so much angst trying to find out what they were that I had to give up the search when I awarded myself that 'holiday from worrying'. I can only assume that they could be literally anything: the sound of a voice, something he has seen on television, a smell perhaps. He doesn't know, any more than we do.

To start off with it was hard to see, but over time we came to realize that there was a definite pattern to Luke's progress. In the very beginning we thought we were getting nowhere. Then we thought we might just be getting somewhere, only to have our hopes dashed. Then we came to see that actually all our hard work was paying off. Luke being able to maintain good behaviour lasted for longer and longer periods of time as his resolve to succeed in life got ever stronger. Although we didn't know what the triggers were we could see when he had been triggered into behaving badly. These days, when he does slip, it seems as though he is 'just a bit off' for a while. We can usually snap him out of it by reminding him how hard he has worked to overcome his difficulties. We tell him that we believe in him and know he can do better and that it is a shame that he has been letting himself down. When he then snaps out of it, it is visible, in that he straightens himself up, as though rising to the challenge. It's as though he grows an inch each time and then he amazes us with his ability to cope, his thoughtfulness and his love for us. He really is a 'scrummy' boy (and of course we think Adam is too).

Adam's development

Adam's advancement, when not being influenced by Luke, was very different. As I said before, he loved to be thought of as the well-behaved one and would do anything to please. It took us quite some time before we realized that this meant that he would use his sneakiness to get Luke into trouble to the extent that it was well worth bearing the pain of one of Luke's thumps to achieve this and get his way. Perhaps we ourselves had planted the idea in his head, but he genuinely seemed to think that if Luke was in trouble, he would be the favourite in our eyes. Thinking about this further, I remembered a time, literally days after he had moved in: the boys were playing in the lounge whilst I was preparing dinner. From the kitchen I heard a loud 'thwack' sound, followed by floods of tears from Adam. It really isn't hard to imagine what happened. I rushed into the lounge and scooped Adam up into my arms, comforting him, whilst remonstrating with Luke. I certainly didn't realize it at the time, but as I looked at Adam, he had an odd look on his face, which I couldn't read; it was almost as though he had a glint in his eye!

I had forgotten about that moment until quite recently, when it suddenly popped into my consciousness and I think that in that moment, when I scooped him into my arms, his unconscious mind might have worked out on his behalf that this (getting Luke into trouble by pestering and antagonizing him) was what he needed to do to get my love and attention. Yikes! I realized for myself just how easy it is inadvertently to lead our children into forming those 'conditioned responses'.

Second child syndrome

Reframing this realization I asked myself: what is good about this? I was then able to sit down and have a long talk with Adam and reframe a lot of things for him. First we talked about how he felt that Luke had always been the favourite in Linda's eyes. I was able to point out that it often feels like that when you are the second child to be born and that, in a way, that might be true, as when a lady (any lady, not just Linda) has their first child, the whole experience of pregnancy, giving birth and motherhood is new to them and every experience is normally a delight. It is not surprising that for a lot of women the birth of the second child is not quite so exciting, because she's been through the whole experience before. This doesn't necessarily mean that she will love the second child any less; it just means that the experience doesn't hold the same excitement. Please note that I hastily pointed out that I was the third child to be born in my family and that perhaps the experience of my birth was even less of a thrill. I also pointed out that women wouldn't choose to go through the pain of childbirth if they didn't want to have a baby, especially if they already knew what that pain was like, so we were able to deduce from this that Linda definitely wanted Adam. Next I pointed out that the mother (any mother) has known the first child longer and, because of this, it may well appear that Linda liked Luke better. I also explained how the mother is aware that her firstborn has been used to having all of her attention and is very conscious that the firstborn might feel left out when she has to focus her attention on the newborn child, as it is the newborn child who needs her attention most.

Adam found all this quite helpful, but was absolutely thrilled by what I pointed out to him next, which was that, of course, when Chris and I chose to adopt two boys, we didn't take Luke and then 18 months later choose Adam. We chose them both at exactly the same time. We didn't have all that time to get to know Luke better; we got to know them at exactly the same time and we certainly never had, and never would, love or favour one above the other. This was an absolute revelation for Adam.

Knowing and understanding this made a huge difference to him and I would say that it provided a turning point in his life, as since then he has been able to open up and talk about his true feelings with me. I cemented this further by saying that I hoped that he and I would be friends for life. I told him that I hoped we would have the kind of relationship where he could always ask for help when he didn't know what to do and that, even when he was married and had children of his own, I would be a huge part of his life. I hoped that he would come to me and say, 'My wife doesn't understand me', or 'Baby Adam won't stop crying, what do I do?' I told him that I might not always have the answers, but I would always be there for him, to help him work out what he could do.

The boys soon became aware that actually they were quite lucky in comparison to others. They now had a new home and loving, caring parents whereas, had they been born in another country, they might well have suffered a far worse fate. I purposely let them see Children in Need and Comic Relief on television and they agreed that we are fortunate in this country even to have a system that picks up on the needs of abused and neglected children. I have always encouraged them to give to charity and we regularly sort out their toys and clothes and donate them to a worthy cause. They were horrified when I told them that a foster parent friend of mine had taken in a new boy who hadn't got any toys of his own. They quickly sorted out a couple of boxes of toys for him and really enjoyed the thought that they were helping someone less fortunate than them. I find it is really sweet when, unprompted, they take money from their own money boxes to donate to charity.

We were pleased to note that the boys started empathizing quite quickly and started noticing when others were ill or needed help. It is amazing how resilient they are and how quickly they put into practice what we teach. Clearly it is not that they didn't want to behave nicely, it is just that they didn't know how, and with a lot of the things we have taught them they didn't even know such ways of being existed. They were often shocked when I pointed out the effect their behaviour was having on other people and they started to notice when other children were naughty. They decided that they weren't going to behave like that, or be rude and disrespectful to others. I seized every opportunity to point out the capabilities (or lack of) of younger children and reminded them that they were only *that big* when this happened, or they had to cope with that, which also helped to put things into perspective for them. Of course, it all took time and often they needed reminders, but these days I genuinely believe them when they say something hurtful quickly followed by, 'I didn't mean it. Oh Mum, I didn't mean to hurt you', which I always follow with, 'You just forgot to think'. They really do hate to hurt me now and I am really pleased when they are able to catch themselves out and apologize without a reminder from me.

Using life as a frame of reference

At every opportunity we have used our own lives as a frame of reference as to how they might or could be feeling, by thinking back to similar incidences in our own lives and remembering how we felt when those things happened. Obviously we didn't suffer from abuse and neglect, but for everyday occurrences this has proved invaluable. We often found that their feelings and reactions were completely different to ours, but by doing this we were able to advise them as to how they ought or could be feeling and reacting and were able to say things like, 'If that had happened to me I would probably feel…', or, 'If I had just done that I would want to…' We also seized every opportunity to give them a 'life lesson'. So something might happen and they would get to feel a certain way, but by 'reframing' what happened we were able to get them to see it from a completely different perspective.

So when we were burgled, we asked them how they felt about it. As you would expect, they didn't like the idea that someone had been in our house and rifled through our belongings and taken some of our stuff. It gave them the negative feelings of fear and anger. By 'reframing' this or putting it into a different 'context' they were able to see that it would make them determined that they would never do that to another person and give that person the feelings that we were having. So, from feeling angry and frightened, they then recognized that this burglary had left them with the positive feelings of determination and strength, which in turn heightened their resolve to be better people. I was able to have them see that, to me, although the stuff that we had stolen might have some sentimental value and monetary value, to me stuff is stuff – it comes and it goes, and is usually replaced with other stuff, especially as we have insurance. The memories that we attach to stuff mean little to me as the memories of a person or a place are actually still in my head and no one can steal those.

I then pointed out that I thought the burglar was actually quite considerate because he had broken in through the conservatory door, and instead of leaving the door open for the weather, animals or birds to get in whilst we were away, he had actually propped a large stone against the door to keep it shut and that we were lucky in that respect because not only do some burglars steal, they often trash the house too. I was able to point out that I actually felt sorry for the burglar who was so desperate to find the money to buy drugs that he had sunk to such levels as stealing and that I hoped that while he was in prison (he was caught the next day) he would receive drug rehabilitation. This of course led to a long discussion about drugs – how Linda had used them, the children's own very frightening experiences of being with people who used drugs, and how we would never get involved with the taking of drugs ourselves.

I was able to ask them what they would do and say if they were offered drugs, alcohol or cigarettes. I suggested that they developed a strategy in the form of a few more 'one liners' so that they were prepared for when the inevitable happened and they were offered something they didn't want, along the lines of, 'No thanks, that's not for me, but you carry on if you want'. At the end of this they were able to see that by 'reframing' and putting what started out as a very negative experience into 'context', they were able to have such an in-depth conversation that they felt pretty good about themselves at the end of it.

Likewise, when their school was broken into and covered in graffiti twice in short succession, we discussed the feelings they had and how it made us all more sure that we would never do that. By doing this regularly with whatever life happens to throw at us, they have stopped seeing things as just 'black and white'. They are now able to see that there are 'grey' areas too and they have started to look for ways of 'reframing' and putting things into 'context' as they happen for themselves. In the early stages of using this technique I used to do this for them, to show them how it could work, but now at every opportunity I ask them to think how they might see things differently for themselves.

To drive these points home further, and to start them on the road of developing their own sense of 'who they are', I did an exercise with the boys where I got them to make a list of all the things that they knew they never wanted to do:

- murder
- steal
- take drugs
- bully or hurt someone
- hurt an animal
- cheat
- be a racist
- cause damage to someone else's property
- do graffiti.

I then told them that there may be very rare circumstances where I might be forced to hurt someone, for example if we were being attacked and I was trying to protect them. I might also steal if I couldn't provide food for them (I added this because there were times in Luke's life when he had stolen from Linda's purse to buy food and had also stolen food from shops) but these would only be in extreme circumstances, which of course I hoped would never happen. We then looked at each boy's behaviour and what they needed to focus on and set targets for improvement, which we made into a list which went on the notice board. Please note that these rules need to be stated in the positive as the brain does not pick up and respond to negatives. The word 'will' puts the action into the future, whereas if you say 'I am...' it implies that you are doing/being that now.

Luke's rules

- If I want something I ask for it properly.
- I use good manners when eating.
- If I can't do my homework I ask for help.
- I always read my written work out loud to make sure it makes sense.

- If I start a job I finish it.
- If I do something wrong, I own up.
- I pay attention and focus on the job in hand.
- I think about what I am going to say before I say it.
- I am always polite and respectful to other people.
- I always look for the good in other people.
- I am always gentle around other people.
- I respect other people's property.
- I respect my own property.
- I respect Mum and Dad.
- I am true and honest with myself.
- I keep myself clean and tidy.
- I keep my nose out of other people's conversations and business.
- I easily notice when I have dug myself into a hole and if necessary ask for help to get out of it.

The great thing about having such a list on the wall is that the next time they are naughty you can refer them back to it and they can work out for themselves where they have gone wrong. To reinforce this we made them each a creed, which was based on the creed they had for karate. (I won't include them both as they were very similar.) I got them to learn their creed by heart and shout it out loud.

Luke's creed

- I believe in myself and look deep inside for the right answers.
- I commit to overcoming my problems once and for all.
- I avoid potentially dangerous situations.
- I fake it to make it.
- I tell myself I can.
- Every minute of every day I work towards getting better and better.

- I block out the rest of the world and focus on the task in hand.
- I give each task 110 per cent.
- I am a yellow dot person (taken from the exercise and safe o'meter, about being and looking for safe people to be with).
- I need Mum and Dad.

A few months ago we were really pleased to receive a letter from Luke's head of year, in which he congratulated Luke on his performance at school and that he had received over 150 house points when he was only half way through the school year. It also mentioned how proud we must be of him. This was elaborated upon soon after when we attended his parents' evening and we met with his head of year in person. He told us that Luke was a delight to teach. What he was most impressed with was that Luke had somehow decided for himself that he wasn't going to get into trouble like some of the children and wasn't afraid to say no when they tried to include him in their antics. He was developing into a fine young man with a conscience and beliefs of his own. This was good news for us indeed, as although we hoped that Luke was standing on his own two feet and sticking up for what he believed in, we had no real way of knowing if this was the case. This news did indeed serve to make Chris and me feel proud and know that all our hard work was worth the effort and was paying off.

Chapter 13

Big Steps Forwards

Adam has an incredible memory. An example of this is that on the first of December (which was a few days ago as I write) I gave the boys their Advent calendar as usual. Adam declared that I had bought him exactly the same calendar as last year and then proceeded to tell me what the picture and chocolate would be like when he opened the window. As you can guess, he was right! He also has an incredible capacity to learn lines for a play or a song, and to him learning things like spellings are a breeze. He also seems to have heightened powers of hearing and is very musical, which is possibly because his eyesight is very poor. He can remember all sorts of trivia from years ago, including lines from television programmes, songs and films.

It may surprise you, then, as it does us to know that as soon as we ask him to do something, like go and get something from upstairs, or put something away somewhere, he seems to find this particularly stressful and literally goes to pieces, so much so that we often find things in the most peculiar places. Breaking this process down further, the moment we say, 'Adam, go and…', he will stand up and either attempt to leave the room before listening to what we have to say or literally start pacing round in circles in a state of anxiety. He then starts singing and dancing around as he sets about whatever task we have set him. I can only guess that he is unable to send clear signals, or the wiring is defective, to the part of the brain that deals with short-term memory and instructions.

A few months ago this seemed to worsen, and so I have been focusing on this ever since. I now seem to be making headway with this particular challenge. I started by putting a couple of things into place that seem to be having the desired effect: when I asked him to take something to a certain place, I asked him to visualize and practise in his mind doing the thing I asked him to do. For example, if I wanted him to put his socks away, I asked him to:

- Close his eyes.
- Hear me saying, 'Adam, will you put your socks away please'.
- Then imagine picking them up, walking down the hall, up the stairs and into his bedroom with them.
- Then he visualized opening his sock drawer, to the extent of noticing which hand he would use.
- Then he saw himself making room for them in the drawer and putting them in.
- Then he could close the drawer and come back downstairs.

I then started delivering the instruction in a different way, by saying, 'Adam, in a moment I am going to ask you to take your socks upstairs, but first I want you to visualize yourself doing this...' Yes, this process is long winded, but it did seem to work. This method can be adapted to suit virtually any situation where he needs to remember something important, be it fetching something or remembering to bring something home from school. In my mind, practice makes perfect, so it was important at that time to give him instructions one at a time, even if that meant that I had to repeat the process with him several times if there were a lot of things that needed doing. The next stage was to get him to do two and then more things at the same time and have him remember lists of things. The next step was to have him take things upstairs to put away and bring things back down to me. Likewise, for each lesson at school, I had him visualize writing his homework in his diary, checking that it made sense, asking the teacher for clarification if it wasn't clear and then, and only then, could he put his things away and go to his next lesson.

Coupled with this, I feel that there is a certain amount of laziness attached to making sure that he has, for example, picked up all his games kit after each lesson. It also feels as though there is a certain amount of, 'It doesn't matter, Mum and Dad will buy me some more' going on. He has now lost one football boot (brand new), one PE sock, his gum shield, and one leg-protective pad from karate, plus wrecked his PE bag, school bag and coat by dragging them on the floor, and wrecked three of his school shirts by getting an orange stain on them (I have no idea where that might come from) and lost countless pens, pencils, scissors, etc. I have now imposed a fine in the hope that if I hit him where it hurts, in the pocket, he might start being more responsible with his equipment.

Coping with excitement

We have talked about how Adam seems to get very stressed when we ask him to do something and he has told me this is often because he is over-excited about something, which could be anything from Christmas to playing on the PlayStation. As a way of dealing with this I have asked him to start imagining:

- Putting his hands out in front of him at waist height.
- Then imagining whatever the thing he is excited about as an object or shape in front of him.
- Then I ask him to imagine picking the object or shape up (still with his hands apart at waist height doing a sort of swivel) and putting it on one side.
- I then ask him to focus all his concentration on the job in hand.
- When he has completed the task, I tell him he can go back to being excited again.

I have done this exercise with him several times now and can remind him of this process by mimicking picking something up and putting it on one side. All this seems to be paying off as recently when I started to make sure that he understood an instruction he stopped me and said he wanted to try to do it for himself. This felt a lot like progress to me!

Learning tips

When the boys moved in with us they were both deemed to be between 18 months and two years behind with their school work. There were gaps in their learning, but it is very hard to know specifically what these gaps were. By continuing to give them extra work, persistently supervising their homework and implementing the following learning strategies and the calming techniques already mentioned, they have both not only caught up but are in the top group for some of their subjects and are attaining very acceptable grades and marks in their exams. By concentrating our attention on improving their maths and English skills, which were their most challenging subjects, they have now gained a new confidence which has affected their ability and results in all the other subjects in their curriculum. We made it very clear to them in turn as they started secondary school that starting a new school gave them the opportunity effectively to wipe the slate clean and start again.

After discussion with Luke's head of year we decided that Luke could stop having progress charts (as mentioned earlier in the book) to check his behaviour, and providing that he could keep it up, he need never have them again. We also told the boys that this was their opportunity to prove to themselves and the rest of the world that, despite their terrible beginnings, they could use the knowledge that they were strong enough to overcome their issues and survive. Therefore they were strong enough to prove that they were capable of great things. We pointed out that the number of exam successes achieved goes hand in hand with the amount of choice they would have in future employment and would dictate the kind of life and money they could expect to have. We also made sure that, to avoid them feeling pressured, they knew that we understood and we knew that they could only do the best that they could do, and that their abilities would allow, and that we would continue to love them whatever their results were and futures held. The reality is that Chris and I really don't mind what they end up doing with their lives as long as they turn out to live within the law and are happy. For their sakes all we wish is that they continue to be the best that they can be.

Having said what we wanted to say we quickly introduced them to the following techniques. A good way of remembering what you read is to read it as though you are teaching it and describing it to someone else. Thus you can read a passage, make sense of it in your head and then imagine explaining it to someone else, making sure that they understand it by having them read it back to you before you move on. I have found that both boys love to explain their work to me, which is great, and I do genuinely enjoy these sessions. I am able to give them feedback, input, ask them questions and give encouragement. I also tell them they must learn on their own as I might not always be available to listen and be taught in the future and want them to have the ability to learn without my input. You can have them take this a step further and imagine teaching a whole class of children and have them raise their hands and ask questions and make comments like, 'What I think you mean is…'

Luke has always had trouble with English, in that when asked to write a piece of work, the ideas seem to come to him so quickly that by the time he has scribbled them all down on the page, his sentences don't make sense, he has spelt most of his words wrong and he has missed all the punctuation out. He is then completely confronted by the prospect of sorting his work out and making corrections. Sometimes the task seems so big that he would rather do anything – even a stretch on the stairs is preferred to completing the work. It has taken a lot of effort to get him to slow down and prepare his work in rough first. We have taught him that when writing an essay it is always good to plan it with a mind map to get the ideas flowing. This can start with the title then spread out to the characters and their description, the scene and its description, key words to be included, and the plot, which leads on to the start, middle and end. Then and only then can he start formulating his sentences. We've advised him to concentrate on just getting a few words right at a time and then to check these for spelling and punctuation. When he is satisfied that they are correct, he can then move on to the next few words. The idea is that it is more manageable and less daunting if the work is broken down into small stages, and the more he practises this technique the better he will get. Soon he will be able to write whole sentences and then paragraphs at a time. We then have him check all of his work again, concentrating on whether it makes sense, then again for the spellings and yet again for the punctuation. I am pleased to report that this method is having the desired effect and his writing is improving.

It is interesting and useful to know that if an exam question has a number by it, that this not only indicates the marks allotted for each question, but indicates the number of key words the marker is looking for. So an essay on Henry VIII might include the following key words: 'Tudor', 'the names of his six wives', 'Catholic', 'annulled', 'beheaded', 'survived' and 'son' and be worth 12 marks. I was quite surprised when Adam's teacher told us this at his recent target setting interview. He also said that the examiner wasn't particularly bothered which words went in between these key words. I wished I had known that when I was at school! I was amazed, incredibly impressed and proud to find, when Adam was revising for his recent history exam, that he was not only looking at an essay he had written on the Battle of Hastings and trying to learn it, he was also trying to improve the essay as he went, so that if that question came up, he could then write an improved version of it during the exam. This technique paid off for him as he attained 88 per cent, which in my mind is excellent, especially considering that when he first came to live with us he was deemed to be far behind with his school work.

A good way to learn to spell is to write half the word in blue and half the word in red on a piece of card and hold it by the child's left shoulder. Whilst she looks at it, you can then ask her to, 'Spell the blue letters then spell the red letters'. Repeat this several times then ask her to spell it backwards. If she can't read it backwards at the first attempt, repeat the process.

More sex lessons

When Luke was in his last year of primary school he started to learn about sex. I wasn't happy to let this happen without me adding what I wanted to say as I wanted to make sure that not only did he learn about the 'facts of life', but he also learned about all the moral issues that in my opinion could easily be taught alongside the facts. As Adam is so close to him in age, and knowing that they would talk, I included Adam when I sat them down to talk through their sex education. I started by asking them what they knew, and I was able to put them straight on a few things by going through all the facts. I got the body book out so we could look at the pictures. I then let them ask me whatever questions they wanted and was pleased to find that they were really quite open and unembarrassed to do this.

The lesson I particularly wanted to drive home was that, although they were learning about sex, that didn't mean that their bodies were ready for sex and it especially didn't mean that they could start experimenting with or having sex. I was really firm when I told them it was against the law to have sex until you are 16. I also told them that they oughtn't to have it then unless they are completely ready to be responsible for both their own and their partner's emotions, in that it isn't okay to take a relationship that far unless both people are completely happy with this and are prepared and responsible enough to take precautions to prevent both pregnancy and the spread of disease. I was really pleased that I took the trouble to do this as, with this and subsequent lessons at the senior school, neither boy was ever told that they oughtn't to have sex until they were older. Having spent some considerable time talking to the boys about this, Adam piped up, 'You know, Mum, I don't think I'll bother with all that. When I'm older I'm going to ask my wife if she wants to adopt children, like you and Dad did!' Bless!

Thankfully both boys have decided to hold back from having a girlfriend until they are quite a bit older. They both feel that they want to get stronger in themselves first and concentrate on doing well at school.

Communication and listening

Research suggests that the human retina transmits data to the brain at the rate of ten million bits per second. As information comes into our brain we therefore have to:

- FILTER INFORMATION: by selecting the bits that we want to hear, which might distort and twist the meaning of what happened
- DELETE INFORMATION: as our brains don't have the capacity to take every bit of information on board, we choose the bits that we need
- GENERALIZE INFORMATION: by forming our own conclusions, which is actually the way that we learn.

To demonstrate how our brains delete information you can ask your child to look around the room that you are in and notice all the things that are yellow (check that they did actually do it) then ask them to name all the things they noticed that were red. Another way is to have them close their eyes and tell them not to think of a pink elephant. They will find that in order not to think about a pink elephant they have to think of a pink elephant first. What these exercises show us is that when something happens one person may see what just occurred one way whilst another person will have a completely different interpretation of what happened. The reality is that neither of them may have processed the information in exactly the same way as it actually happened. This may also go a long way towards explaining why Luke and Adam shared and experienced many things in their early lives and yet they have very different interpretations of what happened and have coped with those experiences in very different ways.

I wanted the boys to learn the real value of communicating and listening effectively. I started by asking them to think about how they normally have a conversation. After the initial, 'I just open my mouth and start talking…' they were soon able to break the process down and agree that what they actually did (and I'm afraid this is true of many people) is that while someone is talking to them, they listen to the first few words of their sentence, then before the other person has finished what they are saying, make up the rest of the sentence and concentrate on thinking about how they are going to reply. Some people even have the cheek to finish the other person's sentences out loud. I then asked them to think about and name the feelings they have, when someone does that to them. The person who was speaking gets to feel that they haven't been listened to properly, that it is really rude to have their words twisted into a different meaning from the one they intended, and since their sentences have been finished for them, they will probably feel quite hurt and get agitated. It really isn't hard to see how arguments and even wars break out. Worse than that, the boys admitted that sometimes they shut off completely, especially if they feel they are being lectured to, and I am sure you understand all the problems that can occur as a result of that.

I wrote some sentences on a piece of paper, read one out, then asked them to repeat what I had just said. Neither of them could get all the words exactly as I had said them. I gave them another couple of goes, but they were still unable to repeat the words exactly. I then asked them to remember how they listened the first time they had been on a plane when it was taxiing on to the runway and the air hostess told the passengers about the safety routine. They agreed that, as it had been their first flight, they had really paid attention because it was a new experience for them. I reminded Luke (who had been sitting next to me) that he had even read the instructions and was interested enough to ask me some questions. I then asked them how hard they had listened to the same routine on the return flight a couple of weeks later. They agreed that they had listened, but perhaps not quite as intently as they had heard it before. I then asked them to think how it would be if they made frequent air trips and they agreed that with each flight they would probably listen less intently and would eventually become quite blasé about it. I then asked them to imagine how they would listen if, just as the air hostess was going into the safety routine, they looked out the window and noticed that the engine was on fire. Of course, they agreed they would listen as though their lives depended on it, and perhaps that that would be true. I then went back and read out the original sentence, only this time with them listening with the new distinction of 'the engine being on fire'. This time they were able to repeat the exact words I had said and in the correct order.

Then we looked at how we could listen and speak. I pointed out that human beings are born with two ears and only one mouth, meaning that we ought to pay more attention to how we listen. The only sensible way to have a conversation is to concentrate completely and listen to the exact words that the other person is saying and then clarify them if you need to. A good way to do this is to say, 'So what you are saying is…?', or 'I would like to make sure that I understand the meaning of what you are saying. Am I right in thinking you mean…?' When you are absolutely sure you have clarified that you understood the true meaning of what they said, then and only then can you formulate your reply in your mind, before finally speaking. In a conversation like this, both people get to feel as though they have been properly heard, respect for the other person will grow, and the conversation can then be productive. Many years ago when I first learned this I found the lesson so powerful that I had to slow my speech right down for a while. When I focused really hard on what the other person was saying I would often stumble and stutter when it was my turn to speak. Thankfully this soon passed.

No one likes not to be listened to, so I often find myself asking the boys to repeat what they just said when they don't speak clearly. If they tell me something when I am otherwise occupied and can't give them my full attention, I make a point of going back to it later. Sometimes, however, both boys have been known to play games when speaking. Luke often used to pretend that he could not hear and got us to repeat ourselves, but now we are wiser we say, 'I know that you heard what I just said', or 'Work it out for yourself, Luke'. Both boys tend to mix up their words, often on purpose. At these times we either ignore them completely or remind them to formulate what they want to say properly before opening their mouths. This all takes a huge amount of practice, but they do improve.

The power of language

There are several words that I always avoid or use with extreme caution. I have already mentioned the word 'but'. 'But' negates whatever you say in front of it, so it is all right to use if you are talking about yourself, 'I like the red one, but I prefer the blue'. 'I think I have done this quite well, but I know that I can do better'. If, however, you are talking to another person, be very careful. Think how you would feel if someone were to say to you: 'I think you have done quite well, but…', or, 'I love you darling, but…' It speaks for itself, doesn't it? Think about when you are giving your opinion about something and the other person butts in with, 'Yes, but…' This leaves you feeling as though your opinion doesn't count or is not worthwhile. It would be far better to say, 'I appreciate that that is your opinion and I think…', or 'I respect that that is your opinion and I think…', or 'I agree and…' Have a go at fitting these statements into your everyday conversations. They feel a little odd at first and a little bit stilted but with practice they will have the desired effect.

My next beef is about the word 'should'. The word 'should' *should* in my opinion be removed from the dictionary as it is so often misused. We allow ourselves to beat ourselves up with the word should. 'I *should* know better, I *should* be able to do this…' We allow other people to beat ourselves up: 'You *should* know better; you *should* be able to do this…' and perhaps we may even be guilty of beating other people up with the word 'should'. My answer to statements like these is always, 'Who says I *should*?', or, 'Why *should* I?' You might find your language is far more effective if you replace the word 'should' with *could*. The word *could* is positive and offers possibility, hope and choice.

The word *try* is great if you want to try a piece of cake, but really doesn't instil you with confidence if someone tells you they will *try* to meet you or *try* to do something for you. 'I'll *try* to get round to putting up the shelves today', 'I'll *try* to pay you back the £5 you lent me', 'I'll *try* to be there at six'. To demonstrate this, ask your child to put her arms out to the side at shoulder height. Tell her that you are going to push her arms down while she *tries* to stop you. You will be able to do it with very little resistance. Then tell her to put her arms up again and *stop* you pushing her arms down again. You may be able to do it, depending on the strength of your child, but it will be a lot harder to do. The purpose of this is to demonstrate that the word *try* is wishy-washy; it may or may not have the desired effect. When you give a direct order or make a positive statement, 'I will put up the shelves today', 'I will give you the £5 you lent me tomorrow', the difference is enormous. The person is believable and things really do start to happen. When one of the children says that they will *try*, I always remind them of this exercise and say, 'Not try. *Do*!'

The word *don't* is like holding up a red flag to a bull: '*Don't* step in the poo', '*Don't* swear at me', '*Don't* eat the sweets'. Remember when I said, '*Don't* think of a pink elephant': in order not to think about it you had to think about it first. It is far more effective to give a direct order: 'Walk on the path', or when necessary the word 'stop', followed by the instruction.

Guessing

Luke's therapist introduced us to the benefits of 'guessing' and this has become a distinction in its own right in our house. Guessing how the boys might be feeling at any given time takes away the implication that we are right and they are wrong. It allows us to give them possible options for the way that they are feeling and gives us an 'in' when the shutters go down. 'I guess from the way that you are behaving that you are having a hard time remembering…today', or 'I guess from the look on your face that you might be feeling…at the moment', or 'I guess that you might be feeling…at the moment. Would you like me to help you reframe this…so that you can feel different?'

I have already mentioned that the mind responds only to direct and positive statements. Because of this we are very careful how we use our language. It is always good to talk about the boys' issues as though they have already dealt with them. I tested this theory out on Luke the next time he was naughty and although he immediately saw straight through me he also agreed that it had the desired effect. I did this by saying, 'That problem that you used to have with…', or, 'Remember when you used to…' I would use these kinds of statements even if the event had just happened, the 'implication' being that this was done, dusted and dealt with and was not under any circumstances going to happen or be a problem again.

Likewise we have found that 'implication' is a very powerful distinction. From the moment the boys moved in we have always 'implied' through our speech that they will live their lives in a certain way: they would overcome their issues and meet their challenges, they would catch up and then do well at school, they would go on to university and then get great jobs, they would meet and marry the woman of their dreams and have a family of their own, and they would feel fulfilled, have fantastic and interesting lives and be blissfully happy. By using language to 'imply' in this way tricks the brain into positive action and they accept it as though it is their destiny.

Influencing our moods/states

The way we speak to ourselves has a direct influence over our moods and states. If we choose to talk to ourselves negatively we will produce a negative state. Likewise if we choose to talk to ourselves positively we will find ourselves in a positive and productive state. Therefore, even if we are feeling down, by talking to ourselves and indeed to others positively we can alter our states. The same is true for the way we use our physicality. If we stare at the floor with our shoulders slumped, it will be very difficult to feel good; if we stand up tall and smile, then it is very difficult to feel down.

Our preferred conditioned responses

Knowing this about moods and states opens up a lot of doors for us, as in my opinion this is where the real 'juice' in life is. I believe that we choose our moods and states, though of course this may not be done consciously, and because of this I think that there must be some element of satisfaction to be had from what we choose. For example, I think that we all have a 'preferred conditioned response', a 'way of being', that we feel really comfortable with. It probably stems back to a decision we made about how the world is when we were small or a strategy we developed to see us through difficult times in our lives. I know people who are 'drama queens', others who are 'martyrs', and some people who seem to be constantly ill. One person I know could trace this back to having sick parents when she was small. Because they were always ill, they got all the attention. Her subconscious mind must have picked up on that as it seemed to tell her that to get the attention she craved, she must make herself ill.

Thinking about this with the children I realized that Adam's 'preferred conditioned response' is: 'poor me' – he was the one who was left out and it is the feelings associated with that that are so comforting and familiar to him. Luke's is 'it's not fair', probably reverted to when he is not the centre of attention and getting his own way.

The problem with having these preferred conditioned responses is that we are less than powerful when we choose to run them. In fact it is as if they run and consume us and we can actually get stuck in this state. When we choose positive moods/states, we can be really effective and powerful in life. I often ask myself what the most effective state would be for me to be in to do whatever it is I am doing at the time. I know that my most powerful and efficient state is my 'just do it' state where, rather than let my mind over-analyse and throw up different reasons to stop me in my tracks, I choose to ignore all those thoughts and just 'do' whatever it is I need to do. When the boys play up I am best in my 'coaching state', where I am calm, patient and insightful. Once I explained this concept to the boys, it was then possible to point out when they were running their 'preferred conditioned responses' so that they could see for themselves when they were being less than powerful and could then change their states for themselves.

In the same way as getting stuck in a less than powerful state, I believe that our subconscious sometimes throws up ways for us 'to be' in order to protect us in some way or give us a kind of feeling (such as illness) that actually gives us an excuse not to participate fully in life. It keeps us watching the game of life from the stands, whereas the real juice in life is to be on the pitch fully participating in the game of life. To combat these less than effective states I often close my eyes, get very quiet by concentrating on my breathing, then imagine going into my brain and opening the door to the department/bit of the brain that was responsible for creating this less than effective way of being. I then thank that bit of the brain for working so hard to protect me and tell it that actually that is not what I want right now. What I want is to be in my 'just do it' state. I then ask it to provide a way to support me in having this. Amazingly, as the subconscious brain loves to please, it will then work on your behalf and find ways of providing this.

Confidence boosters

From time to time we all need our confidence boosting, especially when we are faced with doing something that is challenging or out of the norm. I therefore adapted an exercise taken from NLP and combined it with an exercise I did on a course many years ago. Both boys have found performing in school productions difficult. We have been to many nativity plays and school productions to see them perform, only to find that they are barely visible hiding behind everyone else at the back of the stage. Luke trembles at the merest thought of his weekly drama class. So with another school concert looming I did the following exercise with the boys.

Think of a time when you achieved something that you are incredibly proud of. Adam was able to think of three examples which all work perfectly well for the purposes of this exercise:

- Performing at a karate event for the mayor in which he was chosen with two other boys to shout the karate creed, before giving a demonstration with the rest of the display team.
- Being the only one in his class to have the guts to abseil down a cliff on an activity holiday with the school.
- Winning the 800 metres running race at his last sports day.

Before I carry on I would just like to explain how big a deal these achievements were for him. Adam has always been very good at karate. Although initially he seemed a little slow on the uptake, we soon realized that this was because he was perfecting the moves in his mind before trying them out. When he felt that he was ready, he then performed each move perfectly, so it was no surprise to us when he was picked for the display team. What actually brought a tear to our eye was when he volunteered himself to shout the creed, as to do this he had to race ahead of everyone else to the front of the room and also shout louder than everyone else to be heard. As there were about 50 children there this was an achievement in itself, especially if you consider that only a few years ago he would barely speak, let alone be noticed and heard, and used to hide behind me.

When faced with the opportunity of abseiling he was away from home for the very first time. One by one his class mates backed down from the challenge, but when it came to his turn, he decided for himself that he was going to do it, because he knew that he would feel fantastic if he overcame his fear and also because he knew that he might never get another chance to do it.

At his last sports day he was in four events, of which he won three and was second in the other. This was absolutely fantastic, because not only had he never won a race before in his life, but had never come anywhere near (in fact he was usually last). He told me that as he prepared for the race on the starting line he had decided to put into practice all the things that I had been teaching him and really go for it. In the 800 metres he was up against the previous year's winner who was incredibly confident to the extent of boasting that no one else had a chance and, if that wasn't enough, this boy was almost twice his size. They soon left all the other entrants behind and were neck and neck until the last lap, when Adam decided to give himself another pep talk. He told himself that he still had lots of energy left and that he would feel fantastic when he had won it and, to do that, all he needed to do was run faster. So off he went!

When I asked Luke the same question he immediately shouted out, 'The day I was adopted!' This of course was very good to hear. This experience did indeed give him some excellent feelings, just not the ones that I was aiming for, for the purposes of this exercise. With Luke it was a bit harder to find a single positive achievement. Although he was proud of several things, like getting tons of house points and improving his school grades, in his case he too had to use the experience of performing for the mayor, though this probably wasn't so powerful for him, and climbing a rock face on his activity week, though he didn't sound anywhere near as convincing as Adam. If your child can't think of anything at all, it is possible to make an event up and then imagine the feelings or borrow an event from someone else, but this would be less powerful.

- Next you need to close your eyes.
- Then start picturing the event happening just in front of you.
- Make it bright, colourful and big.
- Notice if there were any sounds that were important to you, like the sound of cheering, or hands clapping, or perhaps you could hear the beat of your heart.
- When you are happy that your picture is strong, then step into it and become a part of the scene.
- Remember what was happening all around you, making it bright and bold and loud.
- Then feel all the sensations you had in your body.
- Remember all the emotions you had at that time. The more powerfully your child feels all these things, the more powerful the final result will be.
- Now picture a gold circle about three feet in diameter on the floor in front of you.
- Imagine putting all these feelings and sensations into the circle. You can get your child to mime this and actually name each thing as she puts it in.
- Then when she has finished that, you can ask her to step into the circle and feel all of those emotions and sensations again.

There are now several ways this can be used, but the object of the exercise is that they can put this 'circle of excellence' wherever they choose and by mentally stepping into it they will automatically re-experience the sensations and emotions of the initial event:

- You could ask her to put this somewhere where she walks every day. It is more powerful if you let her mind create the perfect place. When I first did this exercise, I decided to put it on the doormat, so that every time I went in or out of the house I was automatically empowered.

- You could get her to imagine picking the gold circle up, shrinking it down and putting it in her pocket for use as she enters the exam room, on the start line of that race or as she walks out on to the stage.
- Or you could ask her to imagine picking the circle up, shrinking it down and putting it on her wrist, so that she always has it with her. Then each time she needs to boost her confidence, she can do so by squeezing her wrist.

In each case you need to test if it has worked correctly. So ask her to step into it or squeeze her wrist (as appropriate). If it has worked, she will feel instantly empowered. If it hasn't, it's because she didn't identify with the initial event strongly enough and so you need to take her back to that stage again until she gets it and then test it again.

Chapter 14

Final Thoughts

The boys have lived with us now for nearly seven years and for the most part we are all very happy. In fact, even after all this time I still have to pinch myself sometimes (as I am so pleased and excited) to remind myself that I am a mother; I feel so fortunate to have two such lovely boys. Some days are excellent, some good, some challenging, but that can also be said of everyone, I guess, not just parents with adopted kids!

As we watch our boys grow and develop, what is remarkable is their propensity for tolerance and understanding. They haven't forgotten their past and where they came from, and it was never our intention for them to do so; what they have managed to do is to come to terms with it, not have it affect them, or consume them as it used to. In fact they are now able to look back at their lives without the pain, anger and bitterness that used to overwhelm them and have developed a huge capacity for forgiveness. They have learned to use their experiences to show them just how strong they are and to call on that strength and the knowledge that they survived when they need it in their everyday lives. They are able to use their pasts as a frame of reference for how they definitely don't want to live now. As they are entering their teens, they are already facing the questions of: Who am I? Who do I want to be? What are my beliefs? How do I want to live my life?

The 'Who am I?' is crucial. If you can't 'get' who you are, how can you possibly know who you want to be and what you want to do with your life? It is their understanding and realization of their history, the fact that whilst they cannot change their past they can change the very next minute of their existence, and their grasp of this is amazing. They now love the lives that they live; their faces are radiant with happiness and enthusiasm for life. They care deeply about other people and behave responsibly at home, at school and whilst out in the community. People often comment on how polite, well-behaved, charming, thoughtful, etc. they are. They are both adamant and firm that they don't want to be involved with foolish acts and dare to be different in this respect and have learned to walk away from some of their less than responsible peers. They readily tell me of the challenges they have faced in the course of their day and are proud to tell me how they met those challenges, how they stood up to potential bullies and how they turned down offers of cigarettes and the like.

They have huge respect for Chris, me and the extended family and are never slow in telling us how much they love us, admire our abilities and are striving to be like us. What is amazing is that this is how they want and choose to be. They understand all too well that they are responsible for choosing how they live their life and choosing what the consequences of their actions will be. They are full of integrity and fully understand the good feelings associated with knowing they have done the right thing, even when others don't get it, and most importantly of all, they have learned that when you do all of this – when you are true to yourself and your conscience – you can't help but love and approve of yourself.

We obviously cannot predict the future for our children, although like everyone who has kids, we want all the same things for them: good education, employment, to meet a nice partner and so on. At least we know now that they have a fighting chance, yet as with everything they have experienced with us, it is up to them to take *their* chances and create *their* own futures and opportunities.

It is not what happens to you in life that matters, but how you handle what is thrown at you and what you do next that counts!

Adam has matured in recent times and has started to accept responsibility for stuff a child of his age should be doing. He is progressing well at school and generally is a happy-go-lucky sort of chap…

And when I asked Luke about the string in his head today, he replied, 'What string? Oh *that* old string…it's straight now. Yes, very straight now!'

And so life goes on…

Appendix

Training courses attended

Landmark education courses

Nov 1990	Communication course
Feb 1991	The Forum
Apr 1992	Introduction to the Forum Leaders' Programme
Apr 1991	Leadership seminar
Oct 1991	Introduction to the Forum Leader
Nov 1991	Self-expression and Leadership Programme

These, or similar, courses are offered in many countries around the world.

Anthony Robbins courses

Oct 1993	The Tools of Strategic Influence
Oct 1993	Unleash the Power Within

These, or similar, courses are offered in many countries around the world.

Dr Robert Bays courses

Dec 1993	Skills of Power
Dec 1993	Relationships
Dec 1993	Health and the Mind

As far as I know these courses are no longer available.

Social services courses (UK)

Sep 2000	Living with the Effects of Early Trauma, Linda Gilbert
Sep 2000	Early Trauma, Linda Gilbert
Nov 2000	After Adoption, Carolyn Bennett
Nov 2000	Body Language, Paulette Peters
Jan 2001	Child Development, Carolyn Bennett
Feb 2001	Life Story Books, Karen Theobald
Sep 2001	Managing Behaviour - Over 10s, Claire Marshall
Oct 2001	Separation and Loss, Claire Marshall
Dec 2001	I Don't Want to Do It Your Way, Alec Clarke
Mar 2002	Managing Behaviour - Under 10s, Claire Marshall
Oct 2003	Therapeutic Parenting Course, Inge Roberts and Penny Marshall

Tom Mackay courses

Mar 2006	Practitioner Level Training in Neuro Linguistic Programming
Mar 2006	Time Line Temporal Repatterning

NLP courses are offered in many countries around the world.

Books

Archer, C. (1999) *First Steps in Parenting the Child Who Hurts: Tiddlers and Toddlers.* London: Jessica Kingsley Publishers.

Archer, C. (1999) *Next Steps in Parenting The Child Who Hurts: Tykes and Teens.* London: Jessica Kingsley Publishers.

Archer, C. and Gordon, C. (2006) *New Families Old Scripts: A Guide to the Language of Trauma and Attachment in Adoptive Families.* London: Jessica Kingsley Publishers.

Covey, S.R. (1992) *The Seven Habits Of Highly Effective People.* London: Simon and Schuster.

Deepak, C. (1993) *Ageless Body Timeless Mind.* New York: Crown Publishers Inc.

Hay, L.L. (1987) *You Can Heal Your Life.* Camarillo, CA: DeVorss Publications.

Hirst, M. (2005) *Loving and Living with Traumatised Children.* London: BAAF.

Howe, D. (1995) *Attachment Theory for Social Work Practice.* London: Palgrave Macmillan.

Howe, D. (1996) *Adopters on Adoption: Reflections on Parenthood and Childhood.* London: BAAF.

Howe, D. (2005) *Child Abuse and Neglect: Attachment, Development and Intervention.* London: Palgrave Macmillan.

Hughes, D.A. (1998) *Building the Bonds of Attachment: Awakening Love in Deeply Troubled Children.* Lanham, MD: Jason Aronson Inc.

Hughes, D.A. (2000) *Facilitating Developmental Attachment: The Road to Emotional Recovery and Behavioural Change in Foster and Adopted Children.* Lanham, MD: Jason Aronson Inc.

Peale, N.V. (1992) *You Can If You Think You Can.* New York: Simon and Schuster.

Ponder, C. (1983) *Open Your Mind to Prosperity.* Camarillo, CA: DeVorss Publications.

Robbins, A. (1988) *Unlimited Power.* London: Simon and Schuster.

Robbins, A. (1992) *Awaken the Giant Within.* London: Simon and Schuster.

Scott Peck, M. (1978) *The Road Less Travelled.* New York: Simon and Schuster.

Scott Peck, M. (1987) *The Different Drum.* New York: Simon and Schuster.

Websites

Landmark Education

www.landmarkeducation.com

Offers a comprehensive range of courses which are designed to get participants to examine where they are in life, where they want to be and what is holding them back. By unlocking and removing the barriers the aim is for participants to move forward in the direction they truly want to take, and fulfil their real potential.

Anthony Robbins

www.tonyrobbins.com

As America's leading success coach, Anthony has worked with world leaders, politicians, actors, Fortune 500 companies, and people from all walks of life, both as an individual coach and through his extensive list of training courses, seminars, books and CDs which are available in many countries. Both this site and the Landmark Education site above offer extensive personal development training courses (in many countries) which enable us to identify and understand the areas where we (as individuals) get 'stuck' in life and limit ourselves through our own 'limited' knowledge and experiences. Understanding this then frees us up to be and do whatever we choose to be and do.

Catch-point Adoptive Family Support
www.catchpoint.org
Offers therapeutic support through creative arts and play therapies to adoptive families.

Tom Mackay
www.mackaynlpsolutions.co.uk
Offers a range of training courses using Neuro Linguistic Programming principles for success, transformation and to achieve results in all areas of your life.

MIND
www.mind.org.uk
MIND is the leading mental health charity in England and Wales.

Psychology Today
psychologytoday.com
Provides current articles and useful information on where to find a therapist in the USA and Canada.

NAMI (National Alliance on Mental Illness)
www.nami.org
Offers support, training and information on mental health issues across the USA.

Adoption UK
www.adoptionuk.org
Run by and for adoptive parents and foster carers, offering support, advice and a knowledge base throughout the pre- and post-adoption process and thereafter.

BAAF (British Association for Adoption and Fostering)
www.baaf.org.uk
Very similar to Adoption UK.

NCH (National Children's Homes), the Children's Charity
www.nch.org.uk
The NCH is a more mainstream and recognized charity, which aids children from all walks of society who face challenges and difficulties ranging from poverty to abuse.

American Association of Open Adoption Agencies
www.openadoption.org
This site, specifically for the USA, offers information and support for those involved in open adoption.

Index

6971964R00120

Printed in Great Britain
by Amazon.co.uk, Ltd.,
Marston Gate.